Baby Cashsoft Merino / Summerlite DK

Eleven designs for mama and baby by Erika Knight

bloom
at ROWAN

Photography: Georgina Piper

Art Direction: Arabella Harris

Styling: Holly Bruce

Design Layout: Jennifer Stephens

Illustrations: Rosalyn Kennedy

First published in Great Britain in 2021 by Rowan
Flanshaw Lane, Alverthorpe, Wakefield, WF2 9ND, United Kingdom
E-mail: mail@knitrowan.com

British Library Cataloguing in Publications Data
Rowan Yarns
RB002
EAN: 5010484102300

Palette

Baby Cashsoft Merino

Soft to the touch and feather-like on skin.

Snowflake 101	Cream 102	Taupe 104	Silver 106
Baby Blue 107	Puddle *126	Denim 112	Anthracite 120
Duckling *124	Pickles *123	Cecily *125	Sea Green 108
Camel 103	Nutkin *121	Piglet *122	Vintage pink 105

Summerlite DK

A modern matt finish with an extra-soft feel.

White 465	Seashell 466	Mushroom 454	Silvery Blue 468
Favourite Denim 469	Moon *478	Sailor Blue 470	Steel 458
Duckling *476	Pickles *475	Cecily *477	Giggle *479
Linen 460	Nutkin *473	Piglet *474	Pink Powder 472

Colours by Erika Knight

bloom
at ROWAN

Baby Cashsoft Merino / Summerlite DK

Eleven designs for mama and baby by Erika Knight

When you, a friend or a relative are expecting a baby it is a precious period of nurturing and celebration. This is a time when that instinct to create and protect inspires us to pick up our knitting needles, perhaps for the very first time, and to craft something by hand as an expression of love and care. The joy and excitement of a new life creates a rush of enthusiasm and creativity as well as a desire to personalise the event.

This is a considered collection of comfortable pieces for both mama and baby. Made in tried and trusted Rowan favourites Baby Cashsoft Merino and Summerlite DK, designed to be used interchangeably depending on the season or your fibre preference. Modern classic shapes designed to accommodate a changing body and the everyday needs of new mama, with a relaxed, casual aesthetic and practical details including wraps, button openings and high side vents. And for baby, easy to knit, simple projects perfect for gifting, hand me downs, and for mindful crafting whilst waiting for the new arrival.

These knits are made to be lived in.

Collection

Eleven designs for mama and baby

Serendipity

A long sleeve wrap cardigan fashioned for comfort, with side vents and integral tie belt. The back and right front are worked in 2x2 rib, with a contrast wrap over left front and sleeves in stocking stitch.

Jojoba

A long sleeve tunic style sweater with a soft crew neck and fully fashioned detail. Knitted in stocking stitch with contrast 1x1 rib trims and short row shaped shoulders with a three-needle cast off on the outside. The sides are open to the armhole with button fastening.

Dandelion

A sleeveless vest top knitted in stocking stitch, with shaped hem, which is longer at the back, selvedge side edges split to the armhole and 1 x1 rib ties. Soft round neck, and short row shaped shoulders with a three-needle cast off on the outside.

Lark

A substantial wrap shawl knitted in 2 x 2 rib and contrast stocking stitch and reverse stocking stitch bars to give a simple and effective pattern to enhance the asymmetric triangular shape.

Lullaby

A simple crochet blanket worked in treble crochet, made in multi colour stripes or plain.

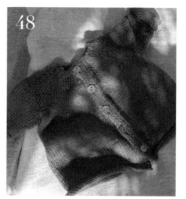

Little Lamb

A simple, seamless 'top down' cardigan with shaped yoke and integral button bands. Turn back cuffs and a roll hem show the contrast reverse stocking stitch to detail.

Bonnie

A little vest top to layer up for warmth and comfort. Knitted in a 2x2 rib with a longer back, a wide neck and with little knitted-in side ties.

Buddy

A basic sweater knitted 'top down' for seamless comfort. Worked in stocking stitch with turn back cuffs, and little roll collar and hem to show the contrast reverse stocking stitch to detail.

Snuggle

Simple, seamless pull-on leggings knitted in the round from the waist to the turn back cuffs. Featuring a wide crotch finished with a three-needle cast off on the outside for comfort.

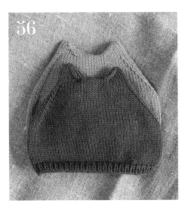

Cherub

A seamless hat knitted in the round with integral shaping to make cute ears. Knitted in stocking stitch with a 1x1 rib trim.

Hush

A pair of seamless little boots worked in stocking stitch and garter stitch with a turnover rib cuff.

Serendipity

pattern page 30

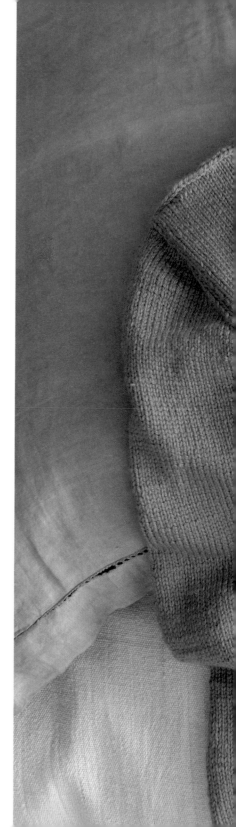

Baby Cashsoft Merino / Summerlite DK

Jojoba

pattern page 36

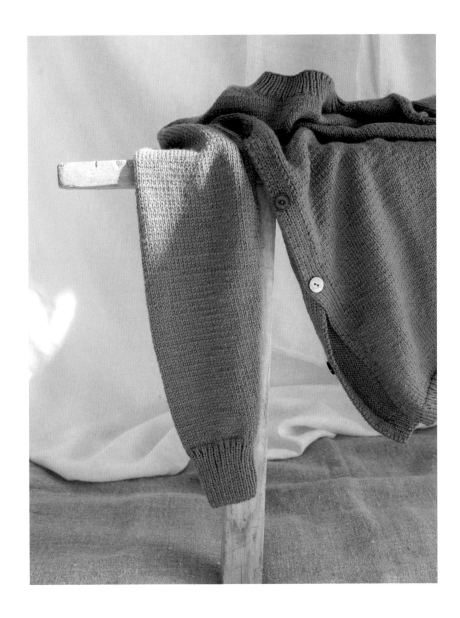

Dandelion

pattern page 40

Baby Cashsoft Merino / Summerlite DK

Lark

pattern page 44

Lullaby

pattern page 46

Baby Cashsoft Merino / Summerlite DK

Little Lamb

pattern page 48

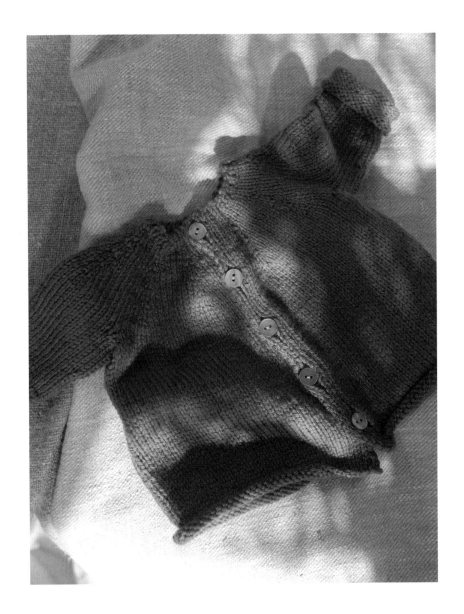

Bonnie

pattern page 50

Baby Cashsoft Merino / Summerlite DK

Buddy and Snuggle

pattern page 52 & 54

Cherub

pattern page 56

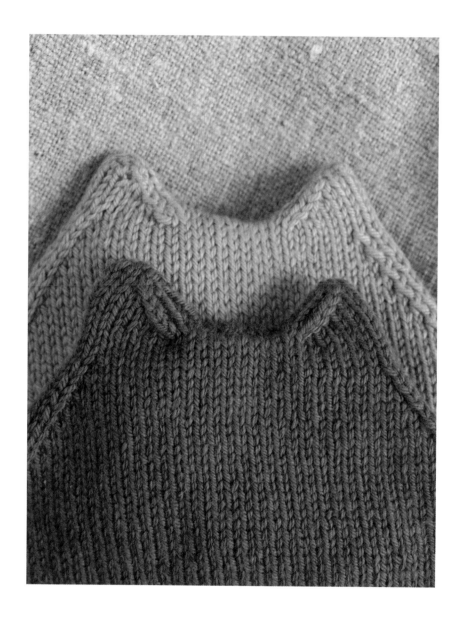

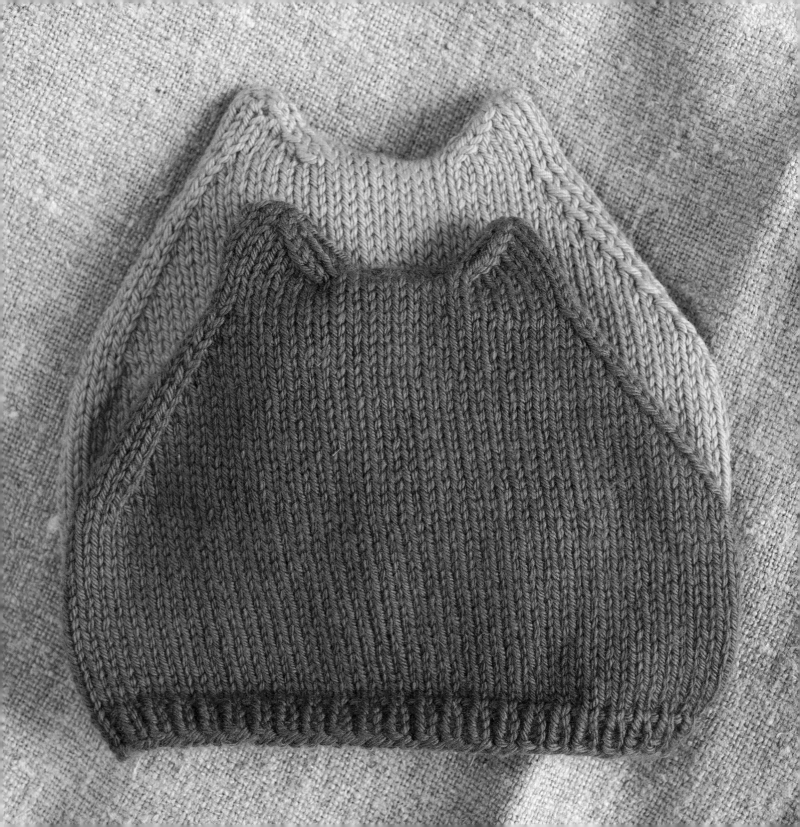

Hush

pattern page 58

Patterns

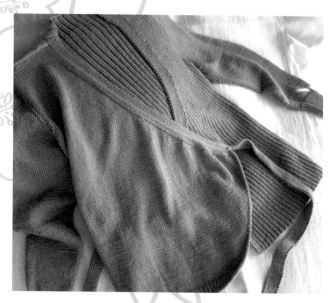

Serendipity ●●○○

SIZE

To fit bust

81-86	91-97	102-107	112-117	122-127	cm
32-34	36-38	40-42	44-46	48-50	in

Actual bust measurement of garment

97.5	108	118.5	128.5	139	cm
38½	42½	46½	50½	54½	in

YARN

Baby Cashsoft Merino

11	13	14	16	17	x 50gm

(photographed in Puddle 126)

NEEDLES

1 pair 3½mm (no 10/9) (US 4) needles, plus one 3½mm (no 10/9) (US 4) needle for casting off shoulders.

TENSION

23 sts and 30 rows to 10 cm measured over st st and rib patt (when stretched) using 3½mm (US 4) needles.

BACK

Using 3½mm (US 4) needles cast on 112 [124: 136: 148: 160] sts. Work in rib patt as folls:

Row 1 (RS): K3, *P2, K2, rep from * to last st, K1.

Row 2: K1, P2, *K2, P2, rep from * to last st, K1.

These 2 rows form rib patt.

Cont in rib patt for a further 64 rows, ending with RS facing for next row.

Place blue markers at both ends of last row to denote top of side seam openings.

Cont in rib patt for further 12 rows, ending with RS facing for next row.

Place a red marker at end of last row to denote base of right side seam tie opening.

Cont in rib patt for a further 16 rows, ending with RS facing for next row.

Place a green marker at end of last row to denote top of right side seam tie opening.

Cont in rib patt for a further 30 [32: 34: 36: 36] rows, ending with RS facing for next row. (Back should meas approx 41.5 [42: 42.5: 43.5: 43.5] cm from cast-on edge.)

Shape armholes

Keeping rib patt correct, cast off 4 sts at beg of next 2 rows. 104 [116: 128: 140: 152] sts.

Next row (RS): K2, sl 1, K1, psso, patt to last 4 sts, K2tog, K2.

Next row: K1, P1, P2tog, patt to last 4 sts, P2tog tbl, P1, K1.

Rep last 2 rows 0 [0: 2: 2: 5] times more. 100 [112: 116: 128: 128] sts.

Next row (RS): K2, sl 1, K1, psso, patt to last 4 sts, K2tog, K2.

Next row: K1, P2, patt to last 3 sts, P2, K1.

Rep last 2 rows 4 [4: 4: 4: 2] times more. 90 [102: 106: 118: 122] sts.

Next row: K3, patt to last 3 sts, K3.

Next row: K1, P2, patt to last 3 sts, P2, K1.

Next row: K2, sl 1, K1, psso, patt to last 4 sts, K2tog, K2. 88 [100: 104: 116: 120] sts.

Cont straight in rib patt for a further 41 [45: 45: 49: 53] rows, ending with RS facing for next row. (Back should meas approx 19.5 [20.5: 22: 23.5: 25.5] cm from beg of armhole shaping.)

Shape shoulders and back neck

Next 2 rows: Patt to last 5 [7: 7: 8: 9] sts, wrap next st (by slipping next st from left needle onto right needle, taking yarn to opposite side of work between needles and then slipping same st back onto left needle – when working back across wrapped sts work the wrapped st and the wrapping loop tog as one st) and turn.

Next 2 rows: Patt to last 10 [14: 14: 17: 18] sts, wrap next st and turn.

Next row: Patt to last 16 [21: 21: 26: 27] sts, wrap next st and turn.

Next row: Patt 6 [7: 8: 9: 9] sts, turn.

Next row: Patt to end, remembering to pick up wrapping loops and working them tog with wrapped sts as you go. 22 [28: 29: 35: 36] sts.

Break yarn leaving a long tail (enough to cast off these sts). Leave these 22 [28: 29: 35: 36] sts on a holder for left shoulder.

With **WS** facing, rejoin yarn to rem 66 [72: 75: 81: 84] sts and patt to last 16 [21: 21: 26: 27] sts, wrap next st and turn.

Next row (RS): Patt 6 [7: 8: 9: 9] sts, turn.

Next row: Patt to end, remembering to pick up wrapping loops and working them tog with wrapped sts as you go. Break yarn and leave these 22 [28: 29: 35: 36] sts on a holder for right shoulder.

Slip rem 44 [44: 46: 46: 48] sts on to a holder.

TIES

Left front tie

Using 3½mm (US 4) needles, cast on 11 sts.

Row 1 (RS): K2, (P1, K1) 4 times, K1.

Row 2: K1, (P1, K1) 5 times.

These 2 rows form rib.

Cont in rib until tie meas 70 [75: 80: 85: 90] cm, ending with **WS** facing for next row.**

Next row (WS): K1, (P1, K1) 4 times, P2tog. 10 sts.

Break yarn and leave these 10 sts on a holder.

Right front tie

Work as given for left front tie to **.

Next row (WS): P2tog tbl, K1, (P1, K1) 4 times. 10 sts.

Do NOT break yarn but leave these 10 sts on a holder (same ball of yarn will be used to complete right front when tie is joined to right front).

LEFT FRONT

Using 3½mm (US 4) needles cast on 112 [124: 136: 148: 160] sts.

Work in rib patt as given for back for 66 rows, ending with RS facing for next row.

Place a blue marker at end of last row to denote top of side seam opening.

Cont in rib patt for further 12 rows, ending with RS facing for next row. (Right front should meas approx 26 cm from cast-on edge.)

Join left front tie and shape front slope

Next row (RS): Patt to last 4 sts, K2tog, K1, P1, then with RS facing, work across 10 sts of left front tie as folls: (K1, P1) 4 times, K2. 121 [133: 145: 157: 169] sts.

Left front tie is now integrated into left front as left front border.

Next row: (K1, P1) 6 times, P2tog, patt to end. 120 [132: 144: 156: 168] sts.

Next row: Patt to last 14 sts, K2tog, (K1, P1) 5 times, K2. 119 [131: 143: 155: 167] sts.

Working front slope decreases and left front border sts as set by last 2 rows, cont as folls:

Dec 1 st at front slope edge of next 43 [45: 47: 49: 49] rows, ending with RS facing for next row. 76 [86: 96: 106: 118] sts.

Shape armhole

Keeping rib patt correct, cast off 4 sts at beg and dec 1 st as before at front slope edge of next row. 71 [81: 91: 101: 113] sts.

Dec 1 st at front slope edge of next row, ending with RS facing for next row. 70 [80: 90: 100: 112] sts.

Working armhole decreases as given for back armhole decreases, dec 1 st at armhole edge of next 3 [3: 7: 7: 13] rows, then on foll 4 [4: 4: 4: 2] alt rows, then on foll 4th row **and at same time** dec 1 st at front slope edge of next 11 [15: 19: 19: 21] rows, then on foll 2 [0: 0: 0: 0] alt rows. 49 [57: 59: 69: 75] sts.

Dec 1 st at front slope edge **only** on 2nd [2nd: next: next: next] and foll 0 [0: 1: 5: 11] rows, then on foll 13 [15: 15: 15: 14] alt rows, then on 2 foll 4th rows, then on foll 6th row, ending with **WS** facing for next row. 32 [38: 39: 45: 46] sts.

Shape shoulder

Next row (WS): Patt to last 5 [7: 7: 8: 9] sts, wrap next st and turn.

Next row: Patt to end.

Next row: Patt to last 10 [14: 14: 17: 18] sts, wrap next st and turn.

Next row: Patt to end.

Next row: Patt to last 16 [21: 21: 26: 27] sts, wrap next st and turn.

Next row: Patt to end.

Next row (WS): K1, (P1, K1) 4 times, inc in next st, then patt to end, remembering to pick up wrapping loops and working them tog with wrapped sts as you go. 33 [39: 40: 46: 47] sts.

Break yarn.

Leave these 33 [39: 40: 46: 47] sts on a holder for left shoulder and left front border.

RIGHT FRONT

Using 3½mm (US 4) needles cast on 64 [76: 88: 100: 112] sts.

Work in rib and shape front opening edge as folls:

Row 1 (RS): K3, *P1, K1, rep from * to last st, K1.

Row 2: K1, *P1, K1, rep from * to last 3 sts, M1P, P2, K1.

Row 3: K3, M1P, *K1, P1, rep from * to last 2 sts, K2. 66 [78: 90: 102: 114] sts.

Rows 4 to 9: As rows 2 and 3, 3 times. 72 [84: 96: 108: 120] sts.

Row 10: K1, *P1, K1, rep from * to last 3 sts, P2, K1.

Cont shaping front opening edge and now work as folls:

Next row (RS): K3, M1, K to end.

Next row: K1, P to end.

These 2 rows set the increases at front opening edge with a K st at right side seam edge on every row and all other sts in st st.

Working all increases as set, inc 1 st at front opening edge of next and foll 26 alt rows. 100 [112: 124: 136: 148] sts.

Work 1 row, ending with RS facing for next row.

Place a blue marker at beg of last row to denote top of side seam opening.

Inc 1 st as before at front opening edge of next and foll 5 alt rows. 106 [118: 130: 142: 154] sts.

Work 1 row, ending with RS facing for next row.

Place a red marker at beg of last row to denote base of right side seam tie opening.

Break yarn.

Join right front tie and shape front slope

Using ball of yarn left at end of right front tie and with RS facing, cont as folls:

Next row (RS): Work across 10 sts of right front tie as folls: K2, (P1, K1) 4 times, then work across right front as folls: K2, sl 1, K1, psso, K to end. 115 [127: 139: 151: 163] sts.

Right front tie is now integrated into right front as right front border.

Next row: K1, P to last 14 sts, P2tog tbl, P3, K1, (P1, K1) 4 times. 114 [126: 138: 150: 162] sts.

Next row: K2, (P1, K1) 3 times, P1, K3, sl 1, K1, psso, K to end. 113 [125: 137: 149: 161] sts.

Working front slope decreases and right front border sts as set by last 2 rows, cont as folls:

Dec 1 st at front slope edge of next 13 rows, ending with RS facing for next row. 100 [112: 124: 136: 148] sts.

Place a green marker at beg of last row to denote top of right side seam tie opening.

Dec 1 st at front slope edge of next 31 [33: 35: 37: 37] rows, ending with **WS** facing for next row. 69 [79: 89: 99: 111] sts.

Shape armhole

Cast off 4 sts at beg and dec 0 [1: 1: 1: 1] st at front slope edge of next row. 65 [74: 84: 94: 106] sts.

Next row (RS): K2, (P1, K1) 3 times, P1, K3, sl 1, K1, psso, K to last 4 sts, K2tog, K2.

Next row: K1, P1, P2tog, P to last 12 [14: 14: 14: 14] sts, (P2tog tbl) 0 [1: 1: 1: 1] time, P3, K1, (P1, K1) 4 times. 62 [70: 80: 90: 102] sts.

Working armhole decreases as set by last 2 rows, dec 1 st at armhole edge of next 1 [1: 5: 5: 11] rows, then on foll 4 [4: 4: 4: 2] alt rows, then on foll 4th row **and at same time** dec 1 st at front slope edge of next 1 [1: 7: 11: 19] rows, then on foll 6 [6: 5: 3: 0] alt rows. 49 [57: 58: 66: 69] sts.

Dec 1 st at front slope edge **only** on 2nd and foll 13 [15: 15: 17: 19] alt rows, then on 2 foll 4th rows. 33 [39: 40: 46: 47] sts.

Work 5 rows, ending with RS facing for next row.

Shape shoulder

Next row (RS): K2, (P1, K1) 3 times, P1, K3, sl 1, K1, psso, K to last 5 [7: 7: 8: 9] sts, wrap next st and turn. 32 [38: 39: 45: 46] sts.

Next row: P to last 9 sts, K1, (P1, K1) 4 times.

Next row: K2, P1, (K1, P1) 3 times, K to last 10 [14: 14: 17: 18] sts, wrap next st and turn.

Next row: P to last 9 sts, K1, (P1, K1) 4 times.

Next row: K2, P1, (K1, P1) 3 times, K to last 16 [21: 21: 26: 27] sts, wrap next st and turn.

Next row: P to last 9 sts, K1, (P1, K1) 4 times.

Next row: K2, P1, (K1, P1) 3 times, inc in next st, K to end, remembering to pick up wrapping loops and working them tog with wrapped sts as you go.

Break yarn leaving a long tail (enough to cast off these sts) and leave these 33 [39: 40: 46: 47] sts on a holder for right front border and right shoulder.

SLEEVES

Using 3½mm (US 4) needles cast on 45 [47: 49: 49: 51] sts.

Row 1 (RS): K1, *P1, K1, rep from * to end.

Row 2: P1, *K1, P1, rep from * to end.

These 2 rows form rib.

Cont in rib until sleeve meas 8.5 cm, ending with RS facing for next row.

Beg with a K row, now work in st st throughout as folls:

Work 6 [6: 4: 4: 4] rows, ending with RS facing for next row.

Next row (RS): K3, M1, K to last 3 sts, M1, K3. 47 [49: 51: 51: 53] sts.

Working all sleeve increases as set by last row, shape sides by inc 1 st at each end of 6th [6th: 4th: 4th: 4th] and every foll 6th [6th: 4th: 4th: 4th] row to 69 [79: 59: 71: 79] sts, then on every foll 8th [-: 6th: 6th: 6th] row until there are 75 [-: 85: 89: 93] sts.

Cont straight until sleeve meas 45 [45: 46: 46: 46] cm, ending with RS facing for next row.

Shape top

Cast off 4 sts at beg of next 2 rows. 67 [71: 77: 81: 85] sts.

Next row (RS): K2, sl 1, K1, psso, K to last 4 sts, K2tog, K2.

Next row: P2, P2tog, P to last 4 sts, P2tog tbl, P2.

Working all sleeve top decreases as set by last 2 rows, dec 1 st at each end of next and foll 2 alt rows, then on 2 [2: 1: 2: 2] foll 4th rows. 53 [57: 65: 67: 71] sts.

Work 1 row.

Dec 1 st at each end of next and every foll alt row until 33 sts rem, then on foll 5 rows, ending with RS facing for next row.

Cast off rem 23 sts.

MAKING UP

Press as described on the information page.

Join right shoulder seam

With RS facing, slip first 11 sts from right front holder onto another holder (right front border), then slip rem 22 [28: 29: 35: 36] sts of right front shoulder onto one 3½mm (US 4) needle, and slip 22 [28: 29: 35: 36] sts of right shoulder of back onto another 3½mm (US 4) needle. Using a 3rd 3½mm (US 4) needle and holding back and right front with their wrong sides together (so that cast-off ridge is on RS of work) and using length of yarn at front shoulder, cast off both sets of shoulder sts together, taking one st from one needle with corresponding st from other needle.

Join left shoulder seam

With RS facing, slip first 22 [28: 29: 35: 36] sts from left front holder onto one 3½mm (US 4) needle for left front shoulder, leaving rem 11 sts on holder (left front border), and slip 22 [28: 29: 35: 36] sts of left shoulder of back onto another 3½mm (US 4) needle. Using a 3rd 3½mm (US 4) needle and holding back and left front with their wrong sides together (so that cast-off ridge is on RS of work) and using length of yarn at back shoulder, cast off both sets of shoulder sts together, taking one st from one needle with corresponding st from other needle.

Back neck border

With RS facing and using 3½mm (US 4) needles, pick up and knit 3 sts down right side of back neck, rib across 44 [44: 46: 46: 48] sts from back neck holder, pick up and knit 3 sts up left side of back neck. 50 [50: 52: 52: 54] sts.
Work 10 rows in rib, taking extra sts into rib patt as set by back.
Cast off in rib.
Graft sts from front borders to row ends of back neck border.
Join left side seam from blue markers at top of side seam opening to beg of armhole shaping.
Join right side seam from blue markers at top of side seam opening to red markers at base of right side seam tie opening.
Join right side seam from green markers at top of right side seam tie opening to beg of armhole shaping.
See information page for finishing instructions, setting in sleeves using the set-in method.

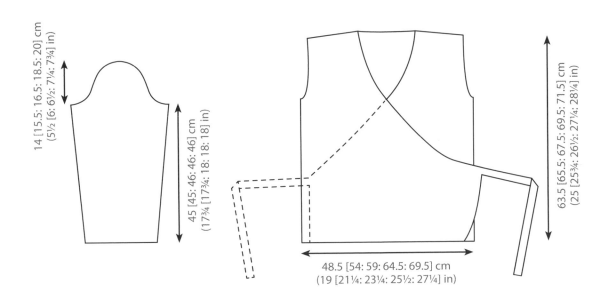

14 [15.5: 16.5: 18.5: 20] cm
(5½ [6: 6½: 7¼: 7¾] in)

45 [45: 46: 46: 46] cm
(17¾ [17¾: 18: 18: 18] in)

63.5 [65.5: 67.5: 69.5: 71.5] cm
(25 [25¾: 26½: 27¼: 28¼] in)

48.5 [54: 59: 64.5: 69.5] cm
(19 [21¼: 23¼: 25½: 27¼] in)

Jojoba ●●○○

SIZE

To fit bust

81-86	91-97	102-107	112-117	122-127	cm
32-34	36-38	40-42	44-46	48-50	in

Actual bust measurement of garment

101.5	112	122.5	131.5	141.5	cm
40	44	48¼	51¾	55¾	in

YARN

Baby Cashsoft Merino

11	13	14	15	16	x 50gm

(photographed in Cecily 125)

NEEDLES

1 pair 3½mm (no 10/9) (US 4) needles, plus one more 3½mm (no 10/9) (US 4) needle for casting off at shoulders. 3¼mm (no 10) (US 3) circular needle no more than 40 cm long

BUTTONS – 10 x grey, 2cm, 2 hole buttons.

TENSION

23 sts and 30 rows to 10 cm measured over st st using 3½mm (US 4) needles.

BACK

Using 3½mm (US 4) needles cast on 127 [139: 151: 161: 173] sts.
Row 1 (RS): K2, *P1, K1, rep from * to last st, K1.
Row 2: K1, *P1, K1, rep from * to end.
These 2 rows form rib.
Cont in rib for a further 8 rows, ending with RS facing for next row.
Now work as folls:
Row 1 (RS): K2, P1, (K1, P1) 3 times, K to last 9 sts, (P1, K1) 3 times, P1, K2.
Row 2: K1, (P1, K1) 4 times, P to last 9 sts, (K1, P1) 4 times, K1.
These 2 rows set the sts – 9 sts at side edges in rib and all other sts in st st.**
Keeping sts correct as set, cont as folls:
Work 130 rows, ending with RS facing for next row.
***Next row (RS):** Cast off 5 sts in rib, K to last 5 sts, cast off last 5 sts in rib.
Break off yarn.
With **WS** facing, rejoin yarn to rem 117 [129: 141: 151: 163] sts and P to end.
Place markers at both ends of last row.
Now completing back in st st throughout and beg with a K row, cont as folls:
Work 6 [8: 10: 12: 14] rows, ending with RS facing for next row. (Back should meas approx 50 [50.5: 51.5: 52: 52.5] cm.)
Shape armholes
Cast off 5 [6: 6: 7: 7] sts at beg of next 2 rows. 107 [117: 129: 137: 149] sts.
Next row (RS): K2, K2tog, K to last 4 sts, K2tog tbl, K2.
Next row: P2, P2tog tbl, P to last 4 sts, P2tog, P2.
Working all armhole decreases as set by last 2 rows, dec 1 st at each end of next 5 [9: 11: 11: 13] rows, then on foll 4 [3: 3: 4: 4] alt rows. 85 [89: 97: 103: 111] sts.***
Cont straight for a further 41 [45: 47: 49: 51] rows, ending with RS facing for next row. (Armhole should meas approx 19.5 [21: 22.5: 24: 25.5] cm.)

Shape shoulders

Next 2 rows: Work to last 3 [3: 4: 5: 5] sts, wrap next st (by slipping next st from left needle onto right needle, taking yarn to opposite side of work between needles and then slipping same st back onto left needle – when working back across wrapped sts work the wrapped st and the wrapping loop tog as one st) and turn.

Next 2 rows: Work to last 6 [7: 8: 10: 10] sts, wrap next st and turn.

Next 2 rows: Work to last 9 [11: 12: 15: 16] sts, wrap next st and turn.

Shape right back neck and shoulder

Next row (RS): K10 [10: 12: 12: 14] and turn, leaving rem sts on a holder. (There should be 19 [21: 24: 27: 30] sts on right needle.)

Work each side of neck separately.

Next row: P3, P2tog tbl, P to last 13 [15: 17: 20: 22] sts, wrap next st and turn. 18 [20: 23: 26: 29] sts.

Next row: K 0 [0: 1: 1: 2], K2tog tbl, K3. 17 [19: 22: 25: 28] sts.

Next row: P to end.

Break yarn leaving a long tail (enough to cast off these sts). Leave these 17 [19: 22: 25: 28] sts on a holder for right shoulder.

Shape left back neck and shoulder

With RS facing, slip centre 47 [47: 49: 49: 51] sts onto a holder (for neckband), rejoin yarn, K to last 13 [15: 17: 20: 22] sts, wrap next st and turn. 19 [21: 24: 27: 30] sts.

Next row (WS): P to last 5 sts, P2tog, P3. 18 [20: 23: 26: 29] sts.

Next row: K3, K2tog, K to end. 17 [19: 22: 25: 28] sts.

Next row: P to end.

Break yarn and leave these 17 [19: 22: 25: 28] sts on a holder for left shoulder.

FRONT

Work as given for back to **.

Keeping sts correct as set, cont as folls:

Work 2 rows, ending with RS facing for next row.

Next row (RS): Rib 4, yfwd, K2tog (to make a buttonhole), rib 3, K to last 9 sts, rib 4, yfwd, K2tog (to make a buttonhole), rib 3.

Work 29 rows.

Rep last 30 rows 3 times more, then work buttonhole row once again (5 sets of buttonholes made).

Work 7 rows, ending with RS facing for next row.

Work as given for back from *** to ***.

Cont straight for a further 29 [33: 33: 35: 35] rows, ending with RS facing for next row.

Shape front neck

Next row (RS): K27 [29: 33: 36: 40] and turn, leaving rem sts on a holder.

Work each side of neck separately.

Next row: P3, P2tog tbl, P to end.

Next row: K to last 5 sts, K2tog tbl, K3.

Working all neck decreases as set by last 2 rows, dec 1 st at neck edge of next 6 rows, then on foll 1 [1: 2: 2: 3] alt rows. 18 [20: 23: 26: 29] sts.

Work 1 row, ending with RS facing for next row.

Shape left shoulder

Next row (RS): K to last 5 sts, K2tog tbl, K3. 17 [19: 22: 25: 28] sts.

Next row: P to last 3 [3: 4: 5: 5] sts, wrap next st and turn.

Next row: K.

Next row: P to last 6 [7: 8: 10: 10] sts, wrap next st and turn.

Next row: K.

Next row: P to last 9 [11: 12: 15: 16] sts, wrap next st and turn.

Next row: K to end.

Next row: P to last 13 [15: 17: 20: 22] sts, wrap next st and turn.

Next row: K to end.

Next row: P to end. 17 [19: 22: 25: 28] sts.

Break yarn leaving a long tail (enough to cast off these sts). Leave these 17 [19: 22: 25: 28] sts on a holder for left shoulder.

With RS facing, slip centre 31 sts onto a holder (for neckband), rejoin yarn and K to end. 27 [29: 33: 36: 40] sts.

Next row: P to last 5 sts, P2tog, P3.

Next row: K3, K2tog, K to end.

Working all neck decreases as set by last 2 rows, dec 1 st at neck edge of next 6 rows, then on foll 1 [1: 2: 2: 3] alt rows. 18 [20: 23: 26: 29] sts.

Work 1 row, ending with RS facing for next row.

Shape right shoulder

Next row (RS): K3, K2tog, K to last 3 [3: 4: 5: 5] sts, wrap next st and turn.

Next row: P to end. 17 [19: 22: 25: 28] sts.

Next row: K to last 6 [7: 8: 10: 10] sts, wrap next st and turn.

Next row: P to end.

Next row: K to last 9 [11: 12: 15: 16] sts, wrap next st and turn.

Next row: P to end.

Next row: K to last 13 [15: 17: 20: 22] sts, wrap next st and turn.

Next row: P to end. 17 [19: 22: 25: 28] sts.

Next row: K to end.

Next row: P to end.

Break yarn and leave these 17 [19: 22: 25: 28] sts on a holder for right shoulder.

SLEEVES

Using 3½mm (US 4) needles cast on 45 [47: 49: 49: 51] sts.

Row 1 (RS): K1, *P1 K1, rep from * to end.

Row 2: P1, *K1, P1, rep from * to end.

These 2 rows form rib.

Cont in rib until sleeve meas 7 cm, ending with RS facing for next row.

Beg with a K row, now work in st st throughout as folls:

Work 6 [6: 6: 4: 4] rows, ending with RS facing for next row.

Next row (RS): K3, M1, K to last 3 sts, M1, K3. 47 [49: 51: 51: 53] sts.

Working all sleeve increases as set by last row, shape sides by inc 1 st at each end of 6th [6th: 6th: 4th: 4th] and every foll 6th [6th: 6th: 4th: 4th] row to 59 [77: 83: 61: 75] sts, then on every foll 8th [8th: -: 6th: 6th] row until there are 73 [79: -: 87: 93] sts.

Cont straight until sleeve meas 45 [45: 46: 46: 46] cm, ending with RS facing for next row.

Shape top

Cast off 5 [6: 6: 7: 7] sts at beg of next 2 rows. 63 [67: 71: 73: 79] sts.

Working all sleeve top decreases in same way as armhole decreases, dec 1 st at each end of next 3 rows, then on foll 2 alt rows, then on 6 [6: 6: 7: 6] foll 4th rows. 41 [45: 49: 49: 57] sts.

Work 1 row.

Dec 1 st at each end of next and every foll alt row until 29 sts rem, then on foll row, ending with RS facing for next row.

Cast off rem 27 sts.

MAKING UP

Press as described on the information page.

Join right shoulder seam as folls:

Slip sts of right shoulder of front onto one 3½mm (US 4) needle, and sts of right shoulder of back onto another 3½mm (US 4) needle. Using a 3rd 3½mm (US 4) needle and holding back and front with their wrong sides together (so that cast-off ridge is on RS of work) and using length of yarn at right back shoulder, cast off both sets of shoulder sts together, taking one st from one needle with corresponding st from other needle.

Join left shoulder seam in same way, using length of yarn at left front shoulder.

note. Join sleeve seams.

Neckband

With RS facing and using 3¼mm (US 3) circular needle, beg at left shoulder seam, pick up and knit 18 [18: 20: 20: 22] sts down left side of front neck, K across 31 sts on front holder, pick up and knit 18 [18: 20: 20: 22] sts up right side of front neck, and 3 sts down right side of back neck, K across 47 [47: 49: 49: 51] sts on back holder, then pick up and knit 3 sts up left side of back neck. 120 [120: 126: 126: 132] sts.

Place marker after last st to denote beg and end of rounds and work as folls:

Round 1 (RS): *K1, P1, rep from * to end.

This round forms rib.

Cont in rib for a further 9 rounds.

Cast off in rib.

Join side seams for 7 [9: 11: 13: 15] rows from markers to beg of armhole shaping. Placing cast-off sts at top of side borders on front over cast-off sts at top of side borders on back, sew cast-off sts in position.

See information page for finishing instructions, setting in sleeves using the set-in method.

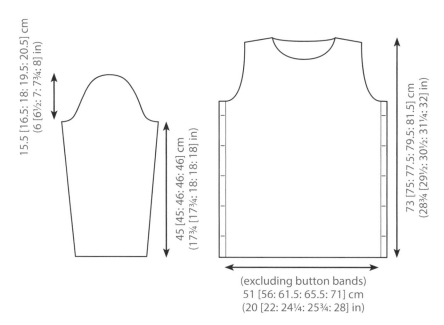

15.5 [16.5: 18: 19.5: 20.5] cm (6 [6½: 7: 7¾: 8] in)

45 [45: 46: 46: 46] cm (17¾ [17¾: 18: 18: 18] in)

73 [75: 77.5: 79.5: 81.5] cm (28¾ [29½: 30½: 31¼: 32] in)

(excluding button bands)
51 [56: 61.5: 65.5: 71] cm
(20 [22: 24¼: 25¾: 28] in)

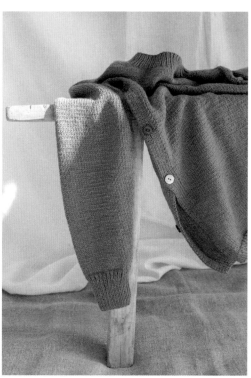

Dandelion ●●○○

SIZE

To fit bust

81-86	91-97	102-107	112-117	122-127	cm
32-34	36-38	40-42	44-46	48-50	in

Actual bust measurement of garment

98	108.5	119	129.5	140	cm
38½	42¾	46¾	51	55	in

YARN

Baby Cashsoft Merino

8	9	10	11	12	x 50gm

(photographed in Nutkin 121)

NEEDLES

1 pair 3½mm (no 10/9) (US 4) needles, plus one more
3½mm (no 10/9) (US 4) needle for casting off at shoulders.
3¼mm (no 10) (US 3) circular needle no more than
40 cm long

TENSION

23 sts and 30 rows to 10 cm measured over st st using
3½mm (US 4) needles.

TIES
Right back tie
Using 3½mm (US 4) needles cast on 9 sts.
Row 1 (RS): K2, (P1, K1) 3 times, K1.
Row 2: K1, (P1, K1) 4 times.
These 2 rows form rib.
Cont in rib until tie meas 60 cm, ending with RS facing for
next row.**
Do NOT break yarn but leave these sts on a holder (same
ball of yarn will be used to complete back when tie is joined
to back).
Left back tie
Work as given for right back tie to **.
Break yarn and leave these sts on a holder.
Left front tie
Work as given for right back tie, noting that this ball of yarn
will be used to complete front when tie is joined to front).
Right front tie
Work as given for right back tie to **.
Break yarn and leave these sts on a holder.

BACK
Using 3½mm (US 4) needles cast on 117 [129: 141: 153: 165] sts.
Row 1 (RS): K2, *P1, K1, rep from * to last st, K1.
Row 2: K1, *P1, K1, rep from * to end.
These 2 rows form rib.
Cont in rib for a further 40 rows, ending with RS facing for
next row.
Now work as folls:
Row 1 (RS): K2, P1, (K1, P1) 3 times, K to last 9 sts, (P1, K1)
3 times, P1, K2.
Row 2: K1, (P1, K1) 4 times, P to last 9 sts, (K1, P1)
4 times, K1.
These 2 rows set the sts – 9 sts at side edges in rib and all
other sts in st st.
Keeping sts correct as set, cont as folls:

Cont straight until back meas 43.5 [44: 44.5: 45: 45.5] cm, ending with RS facing for next row.
Break yarn.

Join ties and shape armholes

With RS of back and **WS** of ties together and using ball of yarn left after completing right back tie, cont as folls:

Next row (RS): K tog first st of right back tie with first st of back, (K tog next st of right back tie with next st of back, P tog next st of right back tie with next st of back) 4 times, work across next 99 [111: 123: 135: 147] sts of back as folls: K2, K2tog, K91 [103, 115: 127: 139], sl 1, K1, psso, K2, then P tog first st of left back tie with next st of back, (K tog next st of left back tie with next st of back, P tog next st of left back tie with next st of back) 3 times, (K tog next st of left back tie with next st of back) twice. 115 [127: 139: 151: 163] sts. **Place markers at both ends of last row to denote base of armhole openings.

Next row: K1, (P1, K1) 4 times, P2, P2tog tbl, P to last 13 sts, P2tog, P2, (K1, P1) 4 times, K1.

Next row: K2, P1, (K1, P1) 3 times, K2, K2tog, K to last 13 sts, sl 1, K1, psso, K2, (P1, K1) 3 times, P1, K2. 111 [123: 135: 147: 159] sts.

Last 2 rows set the sts – 9 sts at side edges in rib and all other sts in st st with armhole decreases worked 11 sts inside each side edge.

Keeping sts correct as set throughout and working all armhole decreases as set by last 2 rows, dec 1 st at each end of next 10 [12: 14: 16: 18] rows, then on foll 4 alt rows. 83 [91: 99: 107: 115] sts.***

Cont straight until armhole meas 19 [20.5: 22: 23.5: 25] cm from markers, ending with RS facing for next row.

Shape shoulders

Next 2 rows: Work to last 5 [5: 6: 7: 8] sts, wrap next st (by slipping next st from left needle onto right needle, taking yarn to opposite side of work between needles and then slipping same st back onto left needle – when working back across wrapped sts work the wrapped st and the wrapping loop tog as one st) and turn.

Next 2 rows: Work to last 9 [10: 12: 14: 16] sts, wrap next st and turn.

Shape right back neck and shoulder

Next row (RS): K9 [12: 13: 15: 16] and turn, leaving rem sts on a holder. (There should be 18 [22: 25: 29: 32] sts on right needle.)

Work each side of neck separately.

Next row: P2tog, P to last 13 [15: 18: 21: 23] sts, wrap next st and turn. 17 [21: 24: 28: 31] sts.

Next row: K to last 2 sts, K2tog. 16 [20: 23: 27: 30] sts.

Next row: P to end, remembering to pick up wrapping loops and working them tog with wrapped sts as you go. 16 [20: 23: 27: 30] sts.

Break yarn leaving a long tail (enough to cast off these sts). Leave these 16 [20: 23: 27: 30] sts on a holder for right shoulder.

Shape left back neck and shoulder

With RS facing, slip centre 47 [47: 49: 49: 51] sts onto a holder (for neckband), rejoin yarn and K to last 13 [15: 18: 21: 23] sts, wrap next st and turn. 18 [22: 25: 29: 32] sts.

Next row (WS): P to last 2 sts, P2tog tbl. 17 [21: 24: 28: 31] sts.

Next row: K2tog tbl, K to end, remembering to pick up wrapping loops and working them tog with wrapped sts as you go. 16 [20: 23: 27: 30] sts.

Next row: P to end.

Break yarn and leave these 16 [20: 23: 27: 30] sts on a holder for left shoulder.

FRONT

Using 3½mm (US 4) needles cast on 105 [117: 129: 141: 153] sts.

Row 1 (RS): K2, *P1, K1, rep from * to last st, K1.

Row 2: K1, *P1, K1, rep from * to end.

These 2 rows form rib.

Keeping sts correct in rib as set, cont as folls:

Row 3: Rib 11, M1, rib to last 11 sts, M1, rib 11.

Work all side increases as set by last row, inc 1 st at each end of 4th and 2 foll 4th rows, taking inc sts into rib. 113 [125: 137: 149: 161] sts.

Work in rib for 1 row more, ending with RS facing for next row.

Now work as folls:

Next row (RS): Rib 9, K to last 9 sts, rib 9.

Next row: Rib 9, P to last 9 sts, rib 9.

These 2 rows set the sts – 9 sts at side edges in rib and all other sts in st st.

Keeping sts correct as set, cont as folls:

Next row (RS): Rib 9, K2, M1, K to last 11 sts, M1, K2, rib 9.

Keeping sts correct as now set throughout and working side increases as set by last row, inc 1 st at each end of 4th row, taking inc sts into st st. 117 [129: 141: 153: 165] sts.

Cont straight until front meas 36.5 [37: 37.5: 38: 38.5] cm, ending with RS facing for next row. (Front should be approx 7 cm shorter than back to beg of armhole shaping.)

Break yarn.

Join ties and shape armholes

With RS of front and **WS** of ties together and using ball of yarn left after completing left front tie, cont as folls:

Next row (RS): K tog first st of left front tie with first st of front, (K tog next st of left front tie with next st of front, P tog next st of left front tie with next st of front) 4 times, work across next 99 [111: 123: 135: 147] sts of front as folls: K2, K2tog, K91 [103, 115: 127: 139], sl 1, K1, psso, K2, then P tog first st of right front tie with next st of front, (K tog next st of right front tie with next st of front, P tog next st of right front tie with next st of front) 3 times, (K tog next st of right front tie with next st of front) twice. 115 [127: 139: 151: 163] sts.

Work as given for back from ** to ***.

Cont straight until 14 [14: 16: 16: 18] rows less have been worked than on back to beg of shoulder shaping, ending with RS facing for next row.

Shape front neck

Next row (RS): Rib 9, K20 [24: 28: 32: 36] and turn, leaving rem sts on a holder. 29 [33: 37: 41: 45] sts.

Work each side of neck separately.

Next row (WS): P2tog, P to last 9 sts, rib 9.

Next row: Rib 9, K to last 2 sts, K2tog. 27 [29: 35: 39: 43] sts.

Keeping sts correct as set and working neck decreases as set by last 2 rows, dec 1 st at neck edge of next 8 rows, then on foll 1 [1: 2: 2: 3] alt rows. 18 [22: 25: 29: 32] sts.

Work 1 row, ending with RS facing for next row.

Shape left shoulder

Next row (RS): K to last 2 sts, K2tog. 17 [21: 24: 28: 31] sts.

Next row: P to last 5 [5: 6: 7: 8] sts, wrap next st and turn.

Next row: K to last 2 sts, K2tog. 16 [20: 23: 27: 30] sts.

Next row: P to last 9 [10: 12: 14: 16] sts, wrap next st and turn.

Next row: K to end.

Next row: P to last 13 [15: 18: 21: 23] sts, wrap next st and turn.

Next row: K to end.

Next row: P to end, remembering to pick up wrapping loops and working them tog with wrapped sts as you go. 16 [20: 23: 27: 30] sts.

Break yarn leaving a long tail (enough to cast off these sts). Leave these 16 [20: 23: 27: 30] sts on a holder for left shoulder.

With RS facing, slip centre 25 sts onto a holder (for neckband), rejoin yarn and K to last 9 sts, rib 9. 29 [33: 37: 41: 45] sts.

Next row (WS): Rib 9, P to last 2 sts, P2tog tbl.

Next row: K2tog tbl, K to last 9 sts, rib 9.

Keeping sts correct as set and working neck decreases as set by last 2 rows, dec 1 st at neck edge of next 8 rows, then on foll 1 [1: 2: 2: 3] alt rows. 18 [22: 25: 29: 32] sts.

Work 1 row, ending with RS facing for next row.

Shape right shoulder

Next row (RS): K2tog tbl, K to last 5 [5: 6: 7: 8] sts, wrap next st and turn. 17 [21: 24: 28: 31] sts.

Next row: P to end.

Next row: K2tog tbl, K to last 9 [10: 12: 14: 16] sts, wrap next st and turn. 16 [20: 23: 27: 30] sts.

Next row: P to end.

Next row: K to last 13 [15: 18: 21: 23] sts, wrap next st and turn.

Next row: P to end.

Next row: K to end, remembering to pick up wrapping loops and working them tog with wrapped sts as you go. 16 [20: 23: 27: 30] sts.

Next row: P to end.

Break yarn and leave these 16 [20: 23: 27: 30] sts on a holder for right shoulder.

MAKING UP

Press as described on the information page.

Using length of yarn at right back shoulder, join right shoulder seam as folls:

Slip sts of right shoulder of front onto one 3½mm (US 4) needle, and sts of right shoulder of back onto another 3½mm (US 4) needle. Using a 3rd 3½mm (US 4) needle and holding back and front with their wrong sides together (so that cast-off ridge is on RS of work), cast off both sets of shoulder sts together, taking one st from one needle with corresponding st from other needle.

Join left shoulder seam in same way, using length of yarn at left front shoulder.

Neckband

With RS facing and using 3¼mm (US 3) circular needle, beg at left shoulder seam, pick up and knit 17 [17: 19: 19: 21] sts down left side of front neck, K across 25 sts on front holder, pick up and knit 17 [17: 19: 19: 21] sts up right side of front neck, and 3 sts down right side of back neck, K across

47 [47: 49: 49: 51] sts on back holder, then pick up and knit 3 sts up left side of back neck. 112 [112: 118: 118: 124] sts.

Place marker after last st to denote beg and end of rounds and work as folls:

Round 1 (RS): *K1, P1, rep from * to end.

This round forms rib.

Cont in rib for a further 14 rounds.

Cast off in rib.

See information page for finishing instructions.

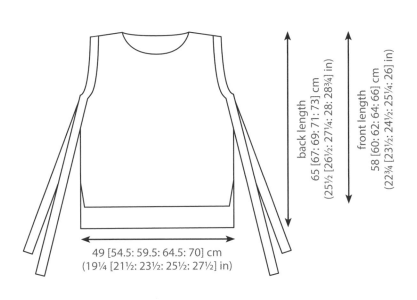

back length
65 [67: 69: 71: 73] cm
(25½ [26½: 27¼: 28: 28¾] in)

front length
58 [60: 62: 64: 66] cm
(22¾ [23½: 24½: 25¼: 26] in)

49 [54.5: 59.5: 64.5: 70] cm
(19¼ [21½: 23½: 25½: 27½] in)

Lark ●○○○

YARN
Baby Cashsoft Merino
    14   x 50gm
(photographed in Pickles 123)

NEEDLES
1 pair 3½mm (no 10/9) (US 4) needles

TENSION
23 sts and 44 rows to 10 cm measured over ridge patt, 28 sts and 30 rows measured over rib patt, both using 3½mm (US 4) needles.

FINISHED SIZE
Completed shawl meas 213 cm (84 in) wide and 88.5 cm (34¾ in) long at deepest point.

SPECIAL ABBREVIATIONS
inc knitwise = K into front then back of next st;
inc purlwise = P into back then front of next st.

SHAWL
Using 3½mm (US 4) needles cast on 2 sts.
Work in ridge patt and shape left side edge as folls:
Row 1 (RS): P2.
Row 2: Inc knitwise in first st, K1. 3 sts.
Row 3: K1, inc knitwise in next st, K1. 4 sts.
Row 4: Purl.
Row 5: P1, inc purlwise in next st, P2. 5 sts.
Row 6: K2, inc knitwise in next st, K2. 6 sts.
Row 7: Knit.
Row 8: P2, inc purlwise in next st, P3. 7 sts.
Now cont shaping left side edge in ridge patt as folls:
Row 9: P to last 3 sts, inc purlwise in next st, P2.
Row 10: Knit.
Row 11: K to last 3 sts, inc knitwise in next st, K2.
Row 12: P2, inc purlwise in next st, P to end.
Row 13: Purl.
Row 14: K2, inc knitwise in next st, K to end.
Row 15: K to last 3 sts, inc knitwise in next st, K2.
Row 16: Purl.
Row 17: P to last 3 sts, inc purlwise in next st, P2.
Row 18: K2, inc knitwise in next st, K to end.
Row 19: Knit.
Row 20: P2, inc purlwise in next st, P to end. 15 sts.
Repeat rows 9 to 20, 20 times more, then repeat rows 9 to 18 once again, ending with RS facing for next row. 182 sts.
Next row (RS): Knit.
Next row: P2, M1P, *(P4, M1P) twice, P5, M1P, rep from * 12 times more, (P4, M1P) twice, P3. 224 sts.
Now work in rib patt and cont shaping left side edge as folls:
Row 1 (RS): K3, *P2, K2, rep from * to last 5 sts, P2, M1, K3. 225 sts.
Row 2: K1, P2, M1P, P1, *K2, P2, rep from * to last st, K1. 226 sts.
Row 3: K3, *P2, K2, rep from * to last 3 sts, M1P, K3. 227 sts.
Row 4: K1, P2, M1, K1, P2, *K2, P2, rep from * to last st, K1. 228sts.
These rows set the rib patt with a knit st at both ends of every row.

Keeping rib patt correct as set and taking inc sts into rib patt, cont shaping left side edge as folls:

Row 5: Rib to last 3 sts, M1, K3.

Row 6: K1, P2, M1P, rib to end.

Row 7: Rib to last 3 sts, M1P, K3.

Row 8: K1, P2, M1, rib to end. 232 sts.

Rep rows 5 to 8, 4 times more. 248 sts.

Work 2 rows straight in rib, ending with RS facing for next row.

Place a marker at beg of last row (to denote deepest point of shawl).

Keeping rib patt correct, now dec at left side edge as folls:

Row 1 (RS): Rib to last 4 sts, K2tog, K2. 247 sts.

Row 2: K1, P2, rib to end.

Rows 3 to 6: As rows 1 and 2 twice more. 245 sts.

Row 7: As row 1.

Row 8: K1, P1, P2tog, rib to end. 243 sts.

Row 9: Rib to last 3 sts, K3.

Rows 10 to 13: As rows 8 and 9 twice more. 241 sts.

Row 14: As row 8. 240 sts.

Rep rows 1 to 14, 29 times more, ending with RS facing for next row. 8 sts.

Next row (RS): K3, P1, K2tog, K2. 7 sts.

Next row: K1, (P2, K1) twice.

Next row: K3, K2tog, K2. 6 sts.

Next row: K1, P4, K1.

Next row: K2, K2tog, K2. 5 sts.

Next row: K1, P3, K1.

Next row: K1, K2tog, K2. 4 sts.

Next row: K1, P2tog, K1. 3 sts.

Next row: K3tog and fasten off.

MAKING UP

Block out shawl to the measurements given, then press carefully with a warm iron over a damp cloth. Leave to dry flat.

See information page for finishing instructions.

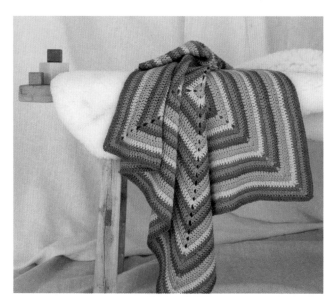

Lullaby ●○○○

YARN
Baby Cashsoft Merino or Summerlite DK
Plain version
     6   x 50gm
(photographed in BCSM Ducking 124)
OR
     6   x 50gm
(photographed in SL DK Moon 478)
Striped version

A	BCSM Pickles 123	1	x 50gm
B	BCSM Duckling 124	1	x 50gm
C	BCSM Cecily 125	1	x 50gm
D	BCSM Puddle 126	2	x 50gm
E	BCSM Nutkin 121	2	x 50gm
F	BCSM Piglet 122	1	x 50gm

CROCHET HOOK
4.50mm (no 7) (US 7) crochet hook

TENSION
First 4 rounds measure 9.5 cm (3¾ in) square using 4.50mm (US 7) crochet hook.

FINISHED SIZE
Completed blanket is approx 66.5 cm (26¼ in) square.

CROCHET ABBREVIATIONS
ch = chain; **ss** = slip stitch; **sp(s)** = space(s); **tr** = treble.

Plain version
Work as given for striped version (below) but using same colour throughout.

Striped version

STRIPE SEQUENCE
Round 1: Using yarn A.
Round 2: Using yarn B.
Round 3: Using yarn C.
Round 4: Using yarn D.
Round 5: Using yarn E.
Round 6: Using yarn F.
These 6 rounds form stripe sequence and are repeated.

BLANKET
Using 4.50mm (US 7) crochet hook and yarn A, make 4 ch and join with a ss to form a ring.
Joining in and breaking off colours as required, cont as folls:
Round 1 (RS): Using yarn A, 5 ch (counts as 1 tr and 2 ch), (3 tr into ring, 2 ch) 3 times, 2 tr into ring, ss to 3rd of 5 ch at beg of round.
Round 2: Using yarn B, ss into first ch sp, 7 ch (counts as 1 tr and 4 ch), 2 tr into ch sp at base of 7 ch, *1 tr into each of next 3 tr**, (2 tr, 4 ch and 2 tr) into next ch sp, rep from * to end, ending last rep at **, 1 tr into ch sp at base of 7 ch at beg of round, ss to 3rd of 7 ch. 44 sts, made up of 7 tr along each side with a 4-ch sp in each corner.
Round 3: Using yarn C, ss into first ch sp, 7 ch (counts as 1 tr and 4 ch), 2 tr into ch sp at base of 7 ch, *1 tr into each of next 7 tr**, (2 tr, 4 ch and 2 tr) into next ch sp, rep

from * to end, ending last rep at **, 1 tr into ch sp at base of 7 ch at beg of round, ss to 3rd of 7 ch. 60 sts, made up of 11 tr along each side with a 4-ch sp in each corner.

Round 4: Using yarn D, ss into first ch sp, 7 ch (counts as 1 tr and 4 ch), 2 tr into ch sp at base of 7 ch, *1 tr into each tr to next corner ch sp**, (2 tr, 4 ch and 2 tr) into next ch sp, rep from * to end, ending last rep at **, 1 tr into ch sp at base of 7 ch at beg of round, ss to 3rd of 7 ch. (4 more tr along each side between corner ch sps.) Last 4 rounds form rounds 1 to 4 of stripe sequence. Beg with stripe sequence round 5, rep round 4, 24 times more, ending after a round using yarn D. (There should be 111 tr along each side between corner ch sps.) Fasten off.

MAKING UP
Press as described on the information page.
See information page for finishing instructions.

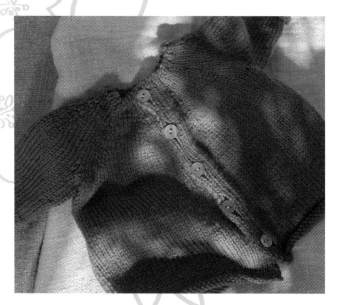

Little Lamb ●●○○

SIZE
To fit age

0-3	3-6	6-9	9-12	months

Actual chest measurement of garment

50.5	54	59	61	cm
20	21¼	23¼	24	in

YARN
Baby Cashsoft Merino

2	2	3	3	x 50gm

(photographed in Nutkin 121)

NEEDLES
1 pair 3½mm (UK 10/9) (US 4) needles
Set of four 3½mm (UK 10/9) (US 4) double-pointed needles

BUTTONS – 5 x grey, 1.2cm, 2 hole buttons.

TENSION
23 sts and 30 rows/rounds to 10 cm measured over st st using 3½mm (US 4) needles.

SPECIAL ABBREVIATIONS
M1L = insert left needle from front to back into the horizontal strand between last st worked and next st on left needle, then knit this strand through the back of the loop; **M1R** = insert left needle from back to front into the horizontal strand between last st worked and next st on left needle, then knit this strand through the front of the loop.

BODY (worked downwards beg at neck edge)
Neckband
Using 3½mm (US 4) needles cast on 65 [71: 75: 81] sts.
Row 1 (RS): P1, *K1, P1, rep from * to end.
Row 2: K1, *P1, K1, rep from * to end.
These 2 rows form neckband.
Yoke
Left over right version
Row 1 (RS): P1, K1, yfwd (to make a buttonhole), K2tog, P1, K55 [30: 65: 35], (K2tog, K- [29: -: 34]) 0 [1: 0: 1] times, (P1, K1) twice, P1. 65 [70: 75: 80] sts.
Right over left version
Row 1 (RS): P1, (K1, P1) twice, K55 [30: 65: 35], (K2tog, K- [29: -: 34]) 0 [1: 0: 1] times, P1, K1, yfwd (to make a buttonhole), K2tog, P1. 65 [70: 75: 80] sts.
Both versions
Working buttonholes as set by last row on every foll 14th [16th: 16th: 18th] row from previous buttonhole until 5 buttonholes have been made in total and noting that no further reference will be made to buttonholes, cont as folls:
Row 2 (WS): K1, (P1, K1) twice, P to last 5 sts, (K1, P1) twice, K1.
Row 3: P1, (K1, P1) twice, K to last 5 sts, (P1, K1) twice, P1.
Last 2 rows set the sts – 5 sts in rib at front opening edges and all other sts in st st.
Keeping sts correct as now set, taking inc sts into st st, cont as folls:
Work 1 row, ending with RS facing for next row.
Next row (RS): Rib 5, K3, (M1R, K5) 10 [11: 12: 13] times, M1R, K2, rib 5. 76 [82: 88: 94] sts.
Work 3 rows, ending with RS facing for next row.
Next row: Rib 5, K3, (M1R, K1, M1L, K5) 10 [11: 12: 13] times, M1R, K1, M1L, K2, rib 5. 98 [106: 114: 122] sts.

Work 3 [3: 5: 5] rows, ending with RS facing for next row.
Next row: Rib 5, K4, (M1R, K1, M1L, K7) 10 [11: 12: 13] times, M1R, K1, M1L, K3, rib 5. 120 [130: 140: 150] sts.
Work 3 [5: 5: 5] rows, ending with RS facing for next row.
Next row: Rib 5, K5, (M1R, K1, M1L, K9) 10 [11: 12: 13] times, M1R, K1, M1L, K4, rib 5. 142 [154: 166: 178] sts.
Work 5 rows, ending with RS facing for next row.
Next row: Rib 5, K6, (M1R, K1, M1L, K11) 10 [11: 12: 13] times, M1R, K1, M1L, K5, rib 5. 164 [178: 192: 206] sts.
Work 5 [5: 5: 7] rows, ending with RS facing for next row. (Yoke should meas approx 9.5 [10: 10.5: 11.5] cm from base of neckband.)

Divide for body and sleeves
Next row (RS): Rib 5, K26 [27: 29: 31] for left front, turn and cast on 8 [8: 10: 10] sts for left underarm, turn, slip next 26 [30: 33: 37] sts onto a holder for left sleeve, K50 [54: 58: 60] for back, turn and cast on 8 [8: 10: 10] sts for right underarm, turn, slip next 26 [30: 33: 37] sts onto a holder for right sleeve, then K26 [27: 29: 31], rib 5 for right front. 128 [134: 146: 152] sts.
Cont as set with 5 sts at front opening edges in rib and all other sts in st st for a further 41 [45: 49: 53] rows, ending with RS facing for next row. (Body should meas approx 14 [15.5: 17: 18] cm from underarm cast-on sts.)
Cast off in patt.

SLEEVES
With RS facing and using 3½mm (US 4) double-pointed needles, rejoin yarn and pick up and knit 8 [8: 10: 10] sts from underarm cast-on sts, then K across 26 [30: 33: 37] sts from sleeve holder. 34 [38: 43: 47] sts.
Distribute sts over 3 of the 4 needles and using 4th needle, work in rounds as folls:
Next round (RS): K4 [4: 5: 5], place a marker to denote beg and end of rounds, then K34 [38: 43: 47].
Cont in st st (K every round) throughout as folls:
Work 8 [8: 7: 6] rounds.
Next round: K1, K2tog tbl, K to last 3 sts, K2tog, K1. 32 [36: 41: 45] sts.

Working all decreases as set by previous round, dec 1 st at each end of 10th [8th: 6th: 7th] and 1 [2: 4: 4] foll 10th [8th: 6th: 7th] rounds. 28 [30: 31: 35] sts.
Cont straight for a further 8 [7: 5: 4] rounds. (Sleeve should meas approx 13 [14: 15: 16] cm from underarm pick-up sts.)
Cast off.

MAKING UP
Press as described on the information page.
See information page for finishing instructions.

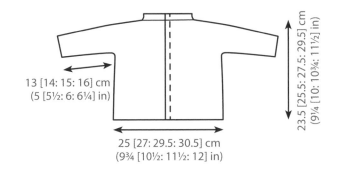

13 [14: 15: 16] cm
(5 [5½: 6: 6¼] in)

23.5 [25.5: 27.5: 29.5] cm
(9¼ [10: 10¾: 11½] in)

25 [27: 29.5: 30.5] cm
(9¾ [10½: 11½: 12] in)

Bonnie ●●○○

SIZE
To fit age

0-3	3-6	6-9	9-12	months

Actual chest measurement of garment

38.5	40	41.5	43.5	cm
15¼	15¾	16¼	17	in

YARN
Baby Cashsoft Merino

1	1	1	2	x 50gm

(photographed in Puddle 126 and Duckling 124)

OR

Summerlite DK

1	1	1	2	x 50gm

(photographed in Moon 478)

NEEDLES
1 pair 3½mm (no 10/9) (US 4) needles
Set of 4 double-pointed 3½mm (no 10/9) (US 4) needles

TENSION
23 sts and 31 rows to 10 cm measured over rib when slightly stretched using 3½mm (US 4) needles.

BACK
Using 3½mm (US 4) needles cast on 44 [46: 48: 50] sts.
Row 1 (RS): K3 [2: 3: 2], *P2, K2, rep from * to last 1 [0: 1: 0] st, K1 [0: 1: 0].
Row 2: P3 [2: 3: 2], *K2, P2, rep from * to last 1 [0: 1: 0] st, P1 [0: 1: 0].
These 2 rows form rib.
Cont in rib until back meas 7 [8.5: 10: 11.5] cm, ending with RS facing for next row. (**For front,** cont until work meas 5 [6.5: 8: 9.5] cm, so that front is 2 cm shorter than back.)
Shape for ties
Next row (RS): Cast on 16 [17: 16: 17] sts, work across these sts and rest of sts as folls: K3, *P2, K2, rep from * to last 1 [0: 1: 0] st, K1 [0: 1: 0].
Next row: Cast on 16 [17: 16: 17] sts, work across these sts and rest of sts as folls: P3, *K2, P2, rep from * to last 1 st, P1. 76 [80: 80: 84] sts.
Cont as set for a further 4 rows, ending with RS facing for next row.
Keeping rib correct **as set by section below ties,** cast off 16 [17: 16: 17] sts at beg of next 2 rows. 44 [46: 48: 50] sts.
Work 2 rows, ending with RS facing for next row.
Next row (RS): K2 [1: 2: 1], sl 1, K1, psso, rib to last 4 [3: 4: 3] sts, K2tog, K2 [1: 2: 1].
Next row: P3 [2: 3: 2], rib to last 3 [2: 3: 2] sts, P3 [2: 3: 2].
Rep last 2 rows 3 times more. 36 [38: 40: 42] sts.**
Cont straight until back meas 16 [18: 20: 22] cm from cast-on edge, ending with RS facing for next row.
Shape back neck
Next row (RS): Rib 7 [7: 8: 8] and turn, leaving rem sts on a holder.
Work each side of neck separately.
Keeping rib correct, dec 1 st at neck edge of next 3 rows, ending with RS facing for next row.
Break yarn and leave rem 4 [4: 5: 5] sts on a holder (for right shoulder seam).
With RS facing, slip centre 22 [24: 24: 26] sts onto a holder (for neckband), rejoin yarn and rib to end.
Keeping rib correct, dec 1 st at neck edge of next 3 rows, ending with RS facing for next row.

Break yarn and leave rem 4 [4: 5: 5] sts on a holder (for left shoulder seam).

FRONT

Noting the bracketed exception (so front is 2 cm shorter than back), work as given for back to **.

Work as given for back until 4 rows less have been worked than on back to beg of back neck shaping, ending with RS facing for next row. (This will be 8 rows below sts left on shoulder holders.)

Shape front neck

Next row (RS): Rib 9 [9: 10: 10] and turn, leaving rem sts on a holder.

Work each side of neck separately.

Keeping rib correct, dec 1 st at neck edge of next 4 rows, then on foll alt row. 4 [4: 5: 5] sts.

Work 1 row, ending with RS facing for next row.

Break yarn, leaving a fairly long end, and leave rem 4 [4: 5: 5] sts on a holder (for left shoulder seam).

With RS facing, slip centre 18 [20: 20: 22] sts onto a holder (for neckband), rejoin yarn and rib to end. 9 [9: 10: 10] sts.

Keeping rib correct, dec 1 st at neck edge of next 4 rows, then on foll alt row. 4 [4: 5: 5] sts.

Work 1 row, ending with RS facing for next row.

Break yarn, leaving a fairly long end, and leave rem 4 [4: 5: 5] sts on a holder (for right shoulder seam).

MAKING UP

Press as described on the information page.

Join shoulder seams as folls: Slip both sets of left shoulder sts onto separate double-pointed needles. Holding RS of back against RS of front and using length of yarn attached to front, cast off both sets of 4 [4: 5: 5] sts together, taking one st from first needle with corresponding st from other needle. Join right shoulder seam in same way.

Neckband

With RS facing and using 3½mm (US 4) double-pointed needles, pick up and knit 8 sts down left side of front neck, 18 [20: 20: 22] sts from front holder, pick up and knit 8 sts up right side of front neck, and 4 sts down right side of

back neck, 22 [24: 24: 26] sts from back holder, then pick up and knit 4 sts up left side of back neck. 64 [68: 68: 72] sts.

Distribute sts over 3 of the 4 needles and using 4th needle, work in rounds as folls:

Round 1 (RS): *K1, P1, rep from * to end.

This round forms rib.

Cont in rib for a further 5 rounds.

Cast off **loosely** in rib. (**Note**: Take great care to ensure cast-off edge is loose enough to fit over baby's head.

If necessary, cast off using a larger size needle.)

See information page for finishing instructions.

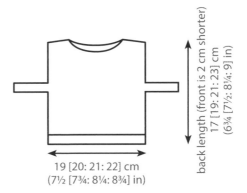

back length (front is 2 cm shorter)
17 [19: 21: 23] cm
(6¾ [7½: 8¼: 9] in)

19 [20: 21: 22] cm
(7½ [7¾: 8¼: 8¾] in)

Buddy ●●○○

SIZE
To fit age

0-3	3-6	6-9	9-12	months

Actual chest measurement of garment

51.5	54	59	61.5	cm
20¼	21¼	23¼	24¼	in

YARN
Baby Cashsoft Merino

2	2	3	3	x 50gm

(photographed in Piglet 122)

NEEDLES
Set of four 3½mm (UK 10/9) (US 4) double-pointed needles
3½mm (UK 10/9) (US 4) circular needle no more than 40 cm long

TENSION
23 sts and 30 rounds to 10 cm measured over st st using 3½mm (US 4) needles.

SPECIAL ABBREVIATIONS
M1L = insert left needle from front to back into the horizontal strand between last st worked and next st on left needle, then knit this strand through the back of the loop; **M1R** = insert left needle from back to front into the horizontal strand between last st worked and next st on left needle, then knit this strand through the front of the loop.

BODY (worked downwards beg at neck edge)
Neckband
Using 3½mm (US 4) double-pointed needles cast on 56 [60: 66: 70] sts LOOSELY.
Distribute sts over 3 of the 4 needles and using 4th needle, work in rounds as folls:
Round 1 (RS): Knit.
This round forms st st.
Place marker in between first and last sts of round just worked to denote beg and end of rounds – this marker denotes centre back.
Cont in st st for a further 4 rounds.
Round 6: *K1, P1, rep from * to end.
This round forms rib.
Cont in rib for a further 5 [5: 7: 7] rounds, dec 1 [0: 1: 0] st at end of last round. 55 [60: 65: 70] sts.
Yoke
Changing to circular needle as required when there are sufficient sts, now work in st st (K every round) as folls:
Work 4 rounds.
Next round: K3, (M1R, K5) 10 [11: 12: 13] times, M1R, K2. 66 [72: 78: 84] sts.
Work 3 rounds.
Next round: K3, (M1R, K1, M1L, K5) 10 [11: 12: 13] times, M1R, K1, M1L, K2. 88 [96: 104: 112] sts.
Work 3 [3: 5: 5] rounds.
Next round: K4, (M1R, K1, M1L, K7) 10 [11: 12: 13] times, M1R, K1, M1L, K3. 110 [120: 130: 140] sts.
Work 3 [5: 5: 5] rounds.
Next round: K5, (M1R, K1, M1L, K9) 10 [11: 12: 13] times, M1R, K1, M1L, K4. 132 [144: 156: 168] sts.
Work 5 rounds.

Next round: K6, (M1R, K1, M1L, K11) 10 [11: 12: 13] times, M1R, K1, M1L, K5. 154 [168: 182: 196] sts.

Work 5 [5: 5: 7] rounds. (Yoke should meas approx 9.5 [10: 10.5: 11.5] cm from base of neckband.)

Divide for body and sleeves

Next round: K26 [27: 29: 31] for right back, turn and cast on 8 [8: 10: 10] sts for right underarm, turn, slip next 26 [30: 33: 37] sts onto a holder for right sleeve, K51 [54: 58: 61] for front, turn and cast on 8 [8: 10: 10] sts for left underarm, turn, slip next 26 [30: 33: 37] sts onto a holder for left sleeve, then K25 [27: 29: 30] for left back. 118 [124: 136: 142] sts.

Cont in st st until body meas 13 [14.5: 16: 17] cm from underarm cast-on sts.

Cast off.

SLEEVES

With RS facing and using 3½mm (US 4) double-pointed needles, rejoin yarn and pick up and knit 8 [8: 10: 10] sts from underarm cast-on sts, then K across 26 [30: 33: 37] sts from sleeve holder. 34 [38: 43: 47] sts.

Work in rounds as folls:

Next round (RS): K4 [4: 5: 5], place a marker to denote beg and end of rounds, then K34 [38: 43: 47].

Cont in st st (K every round) throughout as folls:

Work 8 [8: 7: 6] rounds.

Next round: K1, K2tog tbl, K to last 3 sts, K2tog, K1.

Working all decreases as set by previous round, dec 1 st at each end of 10th [8th: 6th: 7th] and 1 [2: 4: 4] foll 10th [8th: 6th: 7th] rounds. 28 [30: 31: 35] sts.

Cont straight for a further 8 [7: 5: 4] rounds. (Sleeve should meas approx 13 [14: 15: 16] cm from underarm pick-up sts.)

Cast off.

MAKING UP

Press as described on the information page.

See information page for finishing instructions.

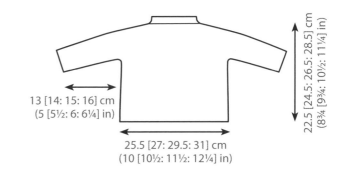

13 [14: 15: 16] cm
(5 [5½: 6: 6¼] in)

22.5 [24.5: 26.5: 28.5] cm
(8¾ [9¾: 10½: 11¼] in)

25.5 [27: 29.5: 31] cm
(10 [10½: 11½: 12¼] in)

Snuggle ●●○○

SIZE
To fit age

| 0-3 | 3-6 | 6-9 | 9-12 | months |

Actual measurement of garment all round waist below rib

| 55 | 56.5 | 58.5 | 60 | cm |
| 21¾ | 22¼ | 23 | 23½ | in |

YARN
Baby Cashsoft Merino

| 2 | 2 | 2 | 3 | x 50gm |

(photographed in Pickles 123)

NEEDLES
3½mm (UK 10/9) (US 4) circular needle no more than 40 cm long
Set of 4 double-pointed 3¼mm (UK 10) (US 3) needles
Set of 4 double-pointed 3½mm (UK 10/9) (US 4) needles

EXTRAS – Length of 2.5 cm (1 in) wide elastic to fit around waist

TENSION
23 sts and 30 rounds to 10 cm measured over st st using 3½mm (US 4) needles.

LEGGINGS (worked downwards from upper edge)
Using 3½mm (US 4) circular needle cast on 118 [122: 126: 130] sts.
Taking care not to twist cast-on edge, work in rounds as folls:
Round 1 (RS): *K1, P1, rep from * to end.
This round forms rib.
Place marker between first and last sts of round just worked to denote beg and end of rounds – this marker denotes right side 'seam'.
Cont in rib until work meas 3 cm.
Next round (RS): Purl – to create foldline.
Cont in rib as before until work meas 6 cm from cast-on edge.
Next round: (K24 [25: 26: 27], M1, K1, M1, K9, M1, K1, M1, K24 [25: 26: 27]) twice. 126 [130: 134: 138] sts.
Now work in st st (K every round) until work meas 21 [22: 23: 24] cm from cast-on edge, ending 22 [23: 24: 25] sts **before** marker.
Divide for legs
Next round (RS): K22 [23: 24: 25], remove marker, K22 [23: 24: 25] and slip rem 82 [84: 86: 88] sts onto a holder.
Cont on these 44 [46: 48: 50] sts for right leg as folls:
**Change to set of 4 double-pointed 3½mm (US 4) needles.
Distribute sts over 3 of the 4 needles and, using 4th needle, work in rounds on these 44 {46: 48: 50] sts for right leg as folls:
Next round (RS): Knit.
Place marker between first and last sts of round just worked to denote beg and end of rounds – this marker denotes inside leg 'seam'.
Work in st st for a further 7 [9: 13: 19] rounds.
Next round (RS): K1, K2tog tbl, K to last 3 sts, K2tog, K1. 42 [44: 46: 48] sts.
Work in st st for a further 3 [4: 6: 9] rounds.
Change to set of 4 double-pointed 3¼mm (US 3) needles.

Work in rib as given for upper edge for 5 cm.
Cast off in rib.
Return to 82 [84: 86: 88] sts on holder and with RS facing, slip first 19 sts onto another holder (for front crotch seam), then rejoin yarn to rem sts and K44 [46: 48: 50], leaving rem 19 sts on holder (for back crotch seam).
Cont on these 44 [46: 48: 50] sts for left leg by working as given for right leg from ** to end.

MAKING UP
Press as described on the information page.
Join crotch seam as folls:
Slip sts on back crotch seam holder onto one double-pointed 3½mm (US 4) needle, and sts on front crotch seam holder onto another double-pointed 3½mm (US 4) needle. Using a third double-pointed 3½mm (US 4) needle and holding back and front crotch seams with their wrong sides together (so that cast-off ridge is on RS of work), cast off both sets of crotch seam sts together, taking one st from one needle with corresponding st from other needle. Around upper edge, fold first 3 cm to inside along foldline and loosely sew in place to form waist casing, leaving an opening for elastic. Thread elastic through this waist casing, join ends and then sew casing opening closed.
See information page for finishing instructions.

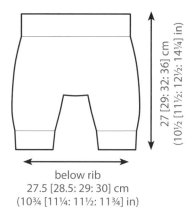

27 [29: 32: 36] cm
(10½ [11½: 12½: 14¼] in)

below rib
27.5 [28.5: 29: 30] cm
(10¾ [11¼: 11½: 11¾] in)

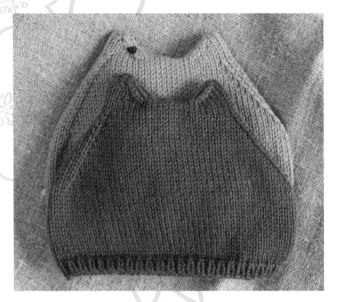

Cherub ●●○○

SIZE

To fit age

| 0-3 | 3-6 | 6-9 | 9-12 | months |

YARN

Baby Cashsoft Merino

| 1 | 1 | 1 | 1 | x 50gm |

(photographed in Pickles 123 and Nutkin 121)

NEEDLES

3¼mm (no 10) (US 3) circular needle no more than 40 cm long
Set of four double-pointed 3¼mm (no 10) (US 3) needles

TENSION

25 sts and 34 rounds/rows to 10 cm measured over st st using 3¼mm (US 3) needles.

HAT

Using 3¼mm (US 3) circular needle cast on 82 [86: 90: 94] sts.
Taking care not to twist cast-on edge, work in rounds as folls:
Round 1 (RS): *K1, P1, rep from * to end.
This round forms rib.
Place marker in between first and last sts of round just worked to denote beg and end of rounds – this marker denotes one side 'seam'.
Cont in rib for a further 3 rounds.
Now work in st st (K every round) until work meas 7.5 [8.5: 9.5: 10.5] cm from cast on edge.
Next round: K41 [43: 45: 47], place another marker, K to end.
There are now 2 markers with 41 [43: 45: 47] sts between markers – each marker denotes a side 'seam'.

Shape crown

Next round: Slip first marker, K1, K2tog tbl, K to 3 sts before second marker, K2tog, K1, slip marker, K1, K2tog tbl, K to 3 sts before first marker, K2tog, K1. 78 [82, 86, 90] sts.
Next round: Knit.
Changing to double-pointed needles as required when the number of sts becomes too few to work on circular needle, rep last 2 rounds 10 times more. 38 [42: 46: 50] sts.
Work in st st for 2 rounds, ending at first marker.

Shape ears

Next round: Remove first marker, K8 [8: 9: 9], cast off next 3 [5: 5: 7] sts, (one st on right needle after cast off), K next 15 [15: 17: 17] sts, removing second marker as you go, then slip these 16 [16: 18: 18] sts onto a holder (for second ear), cast off next 3 [5: 5: 7] sts (one st on right needle after cast-off), K next 7 [7: 8: 8], then K across the 8 [8: 9: 9] sts from beg of round. 16 [16: 18: 18] sts.
Working backwards and forwards in rows, work on these 16 [16: 18: 18] sts for first ear as folls:
**Row 1 (WS): P2, P2tog, P8 [8: 10: 10], P2tog tbl, P2. 14 [14: 16: 16] sts.
Row 2: K2, K2tog tbl, K6 [6: 8: 8], K2tog, K2. 12 [12: 14: 14] sts.
Row 3: P2, P2tog, P4 [4: 6: 6], P2tog tbl, P2. 10 [10: 12: 12] sts.
Row 4: K2, K2tog tbl, K2 [2: 4: 4], K2tog, K2. 8 [8: 10: 10] sts.

Row 5: P2, P2tog, P0 [0: 2: 2], P2tog tbl, P2. 6 [6: 8: 8] sts.
Cast off.
With **WS** facing, rejoin yarn to sts on holder and work
second ear as first ear from ** to end.

MAKING UP
Press as described on the information page.
Join inner ears and crown seam.
See information page for finishing instructions.

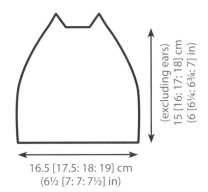

(excluding ears)
15 [16: 17: 18] cm
(6 [6¼: 6¾: 7] in)

16.5 [17.5: 18: 19] cm
(6½ [7: 7: 7½] in)

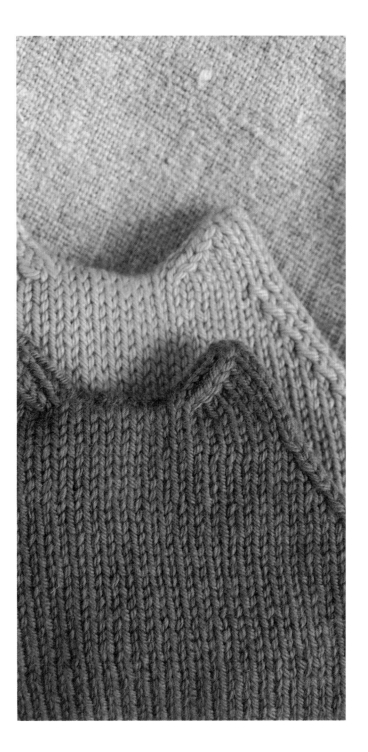

Hush ●●○○

SIZE
To fit age

| 0-3 | 3-6 | 6-9 | 9-12 | months |

YARN
Baby Cashsoft Merino

| 1 | 1 | 1 | 1 | x 50gm |

(photographed in Cecily 125 and Nutkin 121)

NEEDLES
Set of four 3½mm (no 10/9) (US 4) double-pointed needles
Set of four 3¾mm (no 9) (US 5) double-pointed needles

TENSION
23 sts and 30 rounds to 10 cm measured over st st using 3½mm (US 4) needles.

BOOTEES (make 2)
Using 3½mm (US 4) double-pointed needles, cast on 26 [32: 38: 44] sts.
Distribute sts evenly over 3 of the 4 needles and, using 4th needle and taking care not to twist cast-on edge, cont in rounds as folls:
Round 1 (RS): Knit.
This round forms st st.
Place marker in between first and last sts of round just worked to denote beg and end of rounds – this marker denotes centre back of bootee.
Round 2: K2, (M1, K10 [13: 16: 19], M1, K2) twice. 30 [36: 42: 48] sts.
Round 3: Knit.
Round 4: K2, (M1, K12 [15: 18: 21], M1, K2) twice. 34 [40: 46: 52] sts.
Round 5: Knit.
Round 6: K2, (M1, K14 [17: 20: 23], M1, K2) twice. 38 [44: 50: 56] sts.
Round 7: Knit.
Now work in g st as folls:
Round 8: Knit.
Round 9: Purl.
Rep last 2 rounds 4 times more.
Shape foot
Round 1: K17 [20: 23: 26], K2tog tbl, K2tog, K17 [20: 23: 26]. 36 [42: 48: 54] sts.
Round 2: P16 [19: 22: 25], P2tog, P2tog tbl, P16 [19: 22: 25]. 34 [40: 46: 52] sts.
Round 3: K15 [18: 21: 24], K2tog tbl, K2tog, K15 [18: 21: 24]. 32 [38: 44: 50] sts.
Round 4: P14 [17: 20: 23], P2tog, P2tog tbl, P14 [17: 20: 23]. 30 [36: 42: 48] sts.
Round 5: K13 [16: 19: 22], K2tog tbl, K2tog, K13 [16: 19: 22]. 28 [34: 40: 46] sts.
Round 6: P12 [15: 18: 21], P2tog, P2tog tbl, P12 [15: 18: 21]. 26 [32: 38: 44] sts.
Round 7: K11 [14: 17: 20], K2tog tbl, K2tog, K11 [14: 17: 20]. 24 [30: 36: 42] sts.

Round 8: Purl.

Change to 3¾mm (US 5) double-pointed needles.

Work in rib as folls:

Next round: *K1, P1, rep from * to end.

Rep last round 13 [13: 17: 21] times more.

Cast off loosely in rib.

MAKING UP

Press as described on the information page.

Join sole seam.

See information page for finishing instructions.

length of foot
8.5 [9.5: 11: 12] cm
(3¼ [3¾: 4¼: 4¾] in)

Information

TENSION

Obtaining the correct tension is perhaps the single factor which can make the difference between a successful garment and a disastrous one. It controls both the shape and size of an article, so any variation, however slight, can distort the finished garment. Different designers feature in our books and it is their tension, given at the start of each pattern, which you must match. We recommend that you knit a square in pattern and/or stocking stitch (depending on the pattern instructions) of perhaps 5 - 10 more stitches and 5 - 10 more rows than those given in the tension note. Mark out the central 10cm square with pins. If you have too many stitches to 10cm try again using thicker needles, if you have too few stitches to 10cm try again using finer needles. Once you have achieved the correct tension your garment will be knitted to the measurements indicated in the size diagram shown at the end of the pattern.

FINISHING

When you have taken time to craft a garment by hand its important to take care in the pressing and finishing process. Follow the tips below for a truly professional-looking garment.

BLOCKING

Block out each piece of knitting and following the instructions on the ball band press the garment pieces, omitting the ribs. Tip: Take special care to press the edges, as this will make sewing up both easier and neater. If the ball band indicates that the fabric is not to be pressed, then covering the blocked out fabric with a damp white cotton cloth and leaving it to stand will have the desired effect. Darn in all ends neatly along the selvage edge or a colour join, as appropriate.

STITCHING

When stitching the pieces together, remember to match areas of colour and texture very carefully where they meet. Use a seam stitch such as back stitch or mattress stitch for all main knitting seams and join all ribs and neckband with mattress stitch, unless otherwise stated.

CONSTRUCTION

Having completed the pattern instructions, join left shoulder and neckband seams as detailed above. Sew the top of the sleeve to the body of the garment using the method detailed in the pattern.

Set-in sleeves: Place centre of cast-off edge of sleeve to shoulder seam. Set in sleeve, easing sleeve head into armhole.
Join side and sleeve seams.
Slip stitch pocket edgings and linings into place. Sew on buttons to correspond with buttonholes. Ribbed welts and neckbands and any areas of garter stitch should not be pressed.

ABBREVIATIONS

K	knit
P	purl
st(s)	stitch(es)
inc	increas(e)(ing)
dec	decreas(e)(ing)
st st	stocking stitch (1 row K, 1 row P)
g st	garter stitch (K every row)
beg	begin(ning)
foll	following
rem	remain(ing)
rev st st	reverse stocking stitch (1 row K , 1 row P)
rep	repeat
rnd	round
alt	alternate
cont	continue
patt	pattern
tog	together
mm	millimetres
cm	centimetres
in(s)	inch(es)
RS	right side
WS	wrong side
sl 1	slip one stitch
psso	pass slipped stitch over
p2sso	pass 2 slipped stitches over
tbl	through back of loop
M1	make one stitch by picking up horizontal loop before next stitch and knitting into back of it
M1P	make one stitch by picking up horizontal loop before next stitch and purling into back of it
yfwd	yarn forward
yrn	yarn round needle
meas	measures
0	no stitches, times or rows
-	no stitches, times or rows for that size
yo	yarn over needle
yfrn	yarn forward round needle
wyib	with yarn at back
sl2togK	slip 2 stitches together knitways

BUTTONS & RIBBON

Groves & Banks
Eastern Bypass
Thame
Oxfordshire
OX9 3FU
www.grovesltd.co.uk
groves@stockistenquiries.co.uk

Bedecked Haberdashery
The Coach House
Barningham Park
RICHMOND
DL11 7DW
Tel: +44 (0)1833 621 451
eMail:Judith.lewis@bedecked.co.uk
www.bedecked.co.uk

EXPERIENCE RATING
for guidance only

 **Beginner Techniques**

For the beginner knitter, basic garment shaping and straight forward stitch technique.

Simple Techniques

Simple straight forward knitting, introducing various, shaping techniques and garments.

Experienced Techniques

For the more experienced knitter, using more advanced shaping techniques at the same time as colourwork or more advanced stitch techniques.

Advanced Techniques

Advanced techniques used, using advanced stitches and garment shaping along with more challenging techniques.

WASH CARE

To maintain the quality of your precious knits we recommend hand washing in cool water with ultra-gentle Soak Scentless, made from mild, biodegradable, plant-derived ingredients that won't irritate the skin. Simply soak knits for 10-15 minutes, then gently squeeze out the water, roll in a towel to remove any excess moisture, reshape whilst damp and leave to dry flat.

You may have noticed over the last season that the wash care symbols on our ball bands and shade cards have changed. This is to bring the symbols we use up to date and hopefully help you to care for your knitting and crochet more easily. Below are the symbols you are likely to see and a brief explanation of each.

MACHINE WASH SYMBOLS

HAND WASH SYMBOLS

DRY CLEAN SYMBOLS

IRONING SYMBOLS

DO NOT BLEACH SYMBOL

DRYING SYMBOLS

Sizing guide for women

When you knit and wear a Rowan design we want you to look and feel fabulous. This all starts with the size and fit of the design you choose. To help you to achieve a great knitting experience our sizing conforms to standard clothing sizes. Therefore if you buy a standard size 12 in clothing, then our medium patterns will fit you perfectly. The patterns in this book have been designed using integral details with a changing body shape in mind, therefore choose your usual size based on the guide below.

STANDARD WOMENS SIZING GUIDE

The sizing within this chart is also based on the larger size within the range, ie. M will be based on size 14.

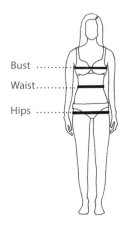

DUAL SIZE	8/10	12/14	16/18	20/22	24/26	
To fit bust	32 – 34	36 – 38	40 – 42	44 – 46	48 – 50	inches
	81 – 86	91 - 97	102 – 107	112 – 117	122 – 127	cm
To fit waist	24 – 26	28 – 30	32 – 34	36 – 38	40 – 42	inches
	61 – 66	71 – 76	81 – 86	91 – 97	102 – 107	cm
To fit hips	34 – 36	38 – 40	42 – 44	46 – 48	50 – 52	inches
	86 – 91	97 – 102	107 – 112	117 – 122	127 – 132	cm

MEASURING GUIDE

For maximum comfort and to ensure the correct fit when choosing a size to knit, please follow the tips below when checking your size.

Measure yourself close to your body, over your underwear and don't pull the tape measure too tight!
Bust/chest – measure around the fullest part of the bust/chest and across the shoulder blades.
Waist – measure around the natural waistline, just above the hip bone.
Hips – measure around the fullest part of the bottom.

If you don't wish to measure yourself, note the size of a favourite jumper that you like the fit of. Our sizes are now comparable to the clothing sizes from the major high street retailers, so if your favourite jumper is a size Medium or size 12, then our size Medium should be approximately the same fit.

To be extra sure, measure your favourite jumper and then compare these measurements with the Rowan size diagram given at the end of the individual instructions.

Finally, once you have decided which size is best for you, please ensure that you achieve the tension required for the design you wish to knit.
Remember if your tension is too loose, your garment will be bigger than the pattern size and you may use more yarn. If your tension is too tight, your garment could be smaller than the pattern size and you will have yarn left over.

Furthermore if your tension is incorrect, the handle of your fabric will be too stiff or floppy and will not fit properly. It really does make sense to check your tension before starting every project.

SIZING & SIZE DIAGRAM NOTE

The instructions are given for the smallest size. Where they vary, work the figures in brackets for the larger sizes. One set of figures refers to all sizes. Included with most patterns in this magazine is a 'size diagram' - see image on the right, of the finished garment and its dimensions. The measurement shown at the bottom of each 'size diagram' shows the garment width 2.5cm below the armhole shaping. To help you choose the size of garment to knit please

refer to the sizing guide. Generally in the majority of designs the welt width (at the cast on edge of the garment) is the same width as the chest. However, some designs are 'A-Line' in shape or have a flared edge and in these cases the welt width will be wider than the chest width.

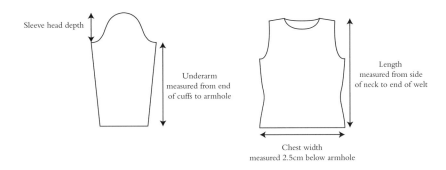

Sizing guide for babies

When you knit a Rowan baby design, we want you to be happy with the look and feel of the finished garment. This all starts with the size and fit of the design you choose. To help you to achieve the correct fit for your baby, please refer to the sizing chart below.

Dimensions in the chart are body measurements, not garment dimensions, therefore please refer to the measuring guide to help you to determine which is the best size for your baby.

STANDARD SIZING GUIDE FOR BABIES

AGE	0-3m	3-6m	6-9 m	9-12 m	
To fit height	22-24.5 56-62	24.5-26.5 62-68	26.5-29 68-74	29-31.5 74-80	in cm
Weight	10-14 4.5-6	14-18 6-8	18-21 8-9.5	21-24 9.5-11	lbs kgs
To fit chest	-	-	-	-	in cm
To fit waist	-	-	-	-	
To fit hips	-	-	-	-	

MEASURING GUIDE

For maximum comfort and to ensure the correct fit when choosing the size to knit, please follow the tips below when checking the size of your baby.
Measure as close to the body over underwear, but don't pull the tape measure too tight!

Height
measure from the top of your baby's head to their feet when they are laying or standing straight.
Chest
measure around the fullest part of the chest and across the shoulder blades.
Waist
measure around the natural waistline just above the hip bone.
Hips
measure around the fullest part of the bottom.

If you don't wish to measure your baby, note the size of their or your favourite jumper that you like the fit of. Our sizes are comparable to the clothing sizes from the major high street retailers, so if the favourite jumper is 6 months, then our 6 months size should measure approximately the same. Measure this favourite jumper and compare the measurements against the size diagram at the end of the pattern you wish to knit.

Finally, once you have decided which size is best for you to knit, please ensure that you achieve the correct tension for the design you are planning to knit.

Remember if your tension is too loose, your garment will be bigger than the pattern size and you may use more yarn. If your tension is too tight, your garment will be smaller than the pattern size and you may have yarn left over. Furthermore if your tension is incorrect, the handle of your fabric will be either too stiff or too floppy and will not fit properly. As you invest money and time in knitting one of our designs, it really does make sense to check your tension before starting your project.

SIZING & SIZE DIAGRAM NOTE

The instructions are given for the smallest size. Where they vary, work the figures in brackets for the larger sizes. One set of figures refers to all sizes. Included with most patterns in this magazine is a 'size diagram' - see image on the right, of the finished garment and its dimensions. The measurement shown at the bottom of each 'size diagram' shows the garment width 2.5cm below the armhole

shaping. To help you choose the size of garment to knit please refer to the sizing guide. Generally in the majority of designs the welt width (at the cast on edge of the garment) is the same width as the chest. However, some designs are 'A-Line' in shape or flared edge and in these cases welt width will be wider than the chest width.

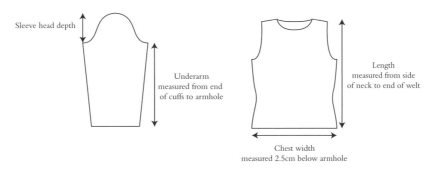

Distributors

AUSTRALIA: Morris and Sons
Level 1, 234 Collins Street, Melbourne Vic 3000
Tel: 03 9654 0888   Web: morrisandsons.com.au

AUSTRALIA: Morris and Sons
50 York Street, Sydney NSW 2000
Tel: 02 92998588   Web: morrisandsons.com.au

AUSTRIA: DMC
5 Avenue de Suisse BP 189, Illzach (France)
Email: info-FR@dmc.com

BELGIUM: DMC
5 Avenue de Suisse BP 189, Illzach (France)
Email: info-FR@dmc.com

CANADA: Sirdar USA Inc.
406 20th Street SE, Hickory, North Carolina, USA 28602
Tel: 828 404 3705   Email: sirdarusa@sirdar.co.uk

CHINA: Commercial Agent Mr Victor Li,
Email: victor.li@mezcrafts.com

CHINA: Shanghai Yujun CO.LTD.
Room 701 Wangjiao Plaza, No.175 Yan'an Road, 200002 Shanghai, China
Tel: +86 2163739785 Email: jessechang@vip.163.com

DENMARK: Carl J. Permin A/S
Egegaardsvej 28 DK-2610 Rødovre
Tel: (45) 36 36 89 89   Email: permin@permin.dk
Web: www.permin.dk

ESTONIA: Mez Crafts Estonia OÜ
Helgi tee 2, Peetri alevik, Tallinn, 75312 Harjumaa
Tel: +372 6 306 759   Email: info.ee@mezcrafts.com
Web: www.mezcrafts.ee

FINLAND: Prym Consumer Finland Oy
Huhtimontie 6, 04200 KERAVA
Tel: +358 9 274871 Email: sales.fi@prym.com

FRANCE: DMC
5 Avenue de Suisse BP 189, Illzach (France)
Email: info-FR@dmc.com

GERMANY: DMC
5 Avenue de Suisse BP 189, Illzach (France)
Email: info-DE@dmc.com

HOLLAND: G. Brouwer & Zn B.V.
Oudhuijzerweg 69, 3648 AB Wilnis
Tel: 0031 (0) 297-281 557   Email: info@gbrouwer.nl

ICELAND: Carl J. Permin A/S
Egegaardsvej 28, DK-2610 Rødovre
Tel: (45) 36 72 12 00   Email: permin@permin.dk
Web: www.permin.dk

ITALY: DMC
Via Magenta 77/5, Rho (Milano)
Email: info-IT@dmc.com

JAPAN: DMC KK
Santo Building 7F,13, Kanda Konya Cho, Chiyodaku, 101-0035 , Tokyo
Email: ouchi@dmc-kk.com

KOREA: My Knit Studio
3F, 59 Insadong-gil, Jongno-gu, 03145, Seoul
Tel: 82-2-722-0006   Email: myknit@myknit.com
Web: www.myknit.com

LATVIA: Latvian Crafts
12-2, Jurģu street, LV-2011
Tel: +371 37 126326825   Email: vjelkins@latviancrafts.lv
Web: www.latviancrafts.lv

LEBANON: y.knot
Saifi Village, Mkhalissiya Street 162, Beirut
Tel: (961) 1 992211   Email: y.knot@cyberia.net.lb

LUXEMBOURG: DMC
5 Avenue de Suisse BP 189, Illzach (France)
Email: info-FR@dmc.com

NEW ZEALAND: Trendy Trims
7 Angle Street, Onehunga, Auckland, New Zealand
Email: trendy@trendytrims.co.nz Web: trendytrims.co.nz

NORWAY: Carl J. Permin A/S
Andersrudveien 1, 1914, Ytre Enebakk
Tel: 23 16 35 30 Email: permin@permin.dk
Web: www.permin.dk

PORTUGAL: DMC
P. Ferrocarriles Catalanes, 117 oficina 34, Cornellá de llobregat, 08940
Email: info-PT @dmc.com

RUSSIA: Family Hobby
Zelenograd, Haus 1505, Raum III, 124683
Email: tv@fhobby.ru   Web: www.family-hobby.ru

SOUTH AFRICA: Arthur Bales LTD
62 4th Avenue, Linden 2195
Tel: (27) 11 888 2401   Email: info@arthurbales.co.za
Web: www.arthurbales.co.za

SPAIN: DMC
P. Ferrocarriles Catalanes, 117 oficina 34, Cornellá de llobregat, 08940
Email: info-SP @dmc.com

SWEDEN: Carl J. Permin A/S
Skaraborgsvägen 35C, 3tr, Borås
Tel: 33 12 77 10 Email: sverige@permin.dk
Web: www.permin.dk

SWITZERLAND: DMC
5 Avenue de Suisse BP 189, Illzach (France)
Email: info-DE@dmc.com

U.S.A.: Sirdar USA Inc
406 20th Street SE, Hickory, North Carolina, USA 28602
Tel: 828 404 3705   Email: sirdarusa@sirdar.co.uk
Web: www.sirdar.com

U.K: Rowan
Flanshaw Lane, Alverthorpe, Wakefield, WF2 9ND, United Kingdom
Tel: 01924 371501   Email: mail@knitrowan.com

For more stockists in all countries please logon to **www.knitrowan.com**

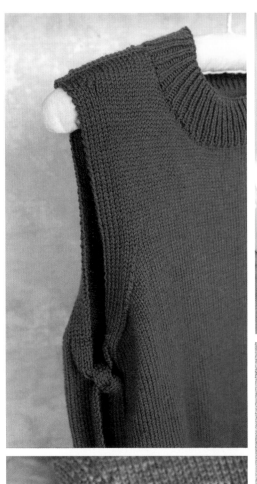
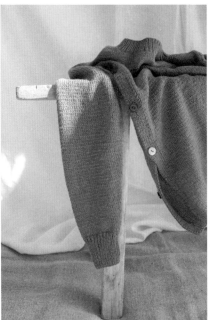

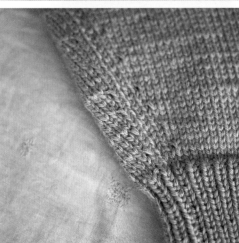